Behind the Mask of the Strong Black Woman

D1566971

Behind the
Mask of the Strong
Black Woman

Voice and the Embodiment of
a Costly Performance

Tamara Beauboeuf-Lafontant

Temple University Press
Philadelphia

05/28/14
ww
$25,95

Temple University Press
1601 North Broad Street
Philadelphia PA 19122
www.temple.edu/tempress

Copyright © 2009 by Temple University
All rights reserved
Published 2009
Printed in the United States of America

∞ The paper used in this publication meets the requirements of the American
National Standard for Information Sciences—Permanence of Paper
for Printed Library Materials, ANSI Z39.48-1992

Library of Congress Cataloging-in-Publication Data

Beauboeuf-Lafontant, Tamara.
Behind the mask of the strong black woman : voice and the embodiment of a costly
performance / Tamara Beauboeuf-Lafontant.
        p. cm.
Includes bibliographical references and index.
ISBN 978-1-59213-667-4 (cloth : alk. paper) — ISBN 978-1-59213-668-1
(pbk. : alk. paper)
1. Women, Black–Psychology.   2. Women, Black–Social conditions.
3. Character.   4. Determination (Personality trait)   I. Title.
HQ1161.B43 2009
155.6'3308996073–dc22

2009005892

2   4   6   8   9   7   5   3   1

For my mother,
Gladys Moïse Beauboeuf,
from whom I first learned
the importance of Black women saying,
"I count, too."

Contents

Behind the Mask of the Strong Black Woman

Introduction

A Half-Told Tale of Black Womanhood

> It is not that Black women have not been and are not strong; it is simply that this is only a part of our story, a dimension, just as the suffering is another dimension—one that has been most unnoticed and unattended to.
>
> —bell hooks, *Talking Back*

The defining quality of Black womanhood is strength. As a reference to tireless, deeply caring, and seemingly invulnerable women, the claim of strength forwards a compelling story of perseverance. Critical figures in this narrative include prominent social activists of the last two centuries, such as Sojourner Truth[1] and Harriet Tubman, Fannie Lou Hamer and Rosa Parks. Each is invoked and revered for embodying a courageous, unselfish commitment to the protection and enfranchisement of the dispossessed. As an account, however, the persuasiveness of strength is not limited to such historical exemplars. Also noted are family members and intimates. Although managing lives of hard, unremunerated, and often low-status work, such mothers and grandmothers have never—as the story goes—attenuated their feminine commitments to the men and children in their lives. Like women in more privileged and protected circumstances, they, too, have been responsible and respectable. This widely accepted tale of who Black women really are also draws us to the attitudes of friends, coworkers, and celebrities who carry themselves with determination and a convincing sense of being "phenomenal" (Angelou 2000) women regardless of their portrayal and treatment by others. In short, strength advances a virtuous claim about any Black woman whose efforts and emotional responses defy common beliefs about what is humanly possible amidst adversity.

And herein lies the problem. Because the idea of strength *appears* to honestly reflect Black women's extensive work and family demands, as well as their accomplishments under far from favorable social conditions, the concept *seems* to provide a simple and in fact honorable recognition of their lives. However, appearances are often deceiving, and much of the acclaim that the concept of strength provides for Black women is undermined by what I argue is its real function: to defend and maintain a stratified social order by obscuring Black women's experiences of suffering, acts of desperation, and anger.

As bell hooks (1989, 153) suggests in the epigraph, strength is a half-told tale. Within this incomplete narrative, "most unnoticed and unattended to" have been Black women's human vulnerabilities. Swept under this cover story are what Black women experience disproportionately—disparagements and violations of their minds and bodies, foreclosed opportunities to experience full citizenship, and social responsibilities that fall to them as people of color, who are women, and too often also poor (see, for example, Duffy 2007; Richie 1995; Roberts 1997; Williams 2002). In a society woven from resilient threads of sexism, racism, and class exploitation, strong Black women occupy a particular discursive and material space. They are required to be, as Zora Neale Hurston (1937, 14) famously described, "de mule[s] uh de world." Their specific function in the script of American social relations—distinct from the roles of other race–gender groups—has been to take on the burdens and complete the tasks that enable society as we know it to continue.

Strength is a "mystique" (Friedan [1963]1983). It derives from the American fascination with self-made personalities and a structurally transcendent, victorious individualism. Thus, strong Black women are important characters in a redemptive narrative or "sincere fiction" (Vera, Feagin, and Gordon 1995) of race, gender, and class relations. As "invented greats" (Irvin Painter 1996), strong Black women embody precisely those qualities that inspire a grossly simplified and thereby sentimental statement about American social reality. To assert the idea of strong Black women during slavery, segregation, or contemporary institutional racism and intra-racial sexism is to maintain a reassuring conviction: that personal actions and agency trump all manner of social abuses. Therefore, the presence of "strong Black women" soothes many a conscience that could be troubled by the material conditions forced upon such persons and the toll of organized injustice on their humanity. In other words, strong Black women do not simply exist, they *play* critical roles in the societal imagination and in social life. It is therefore questionable whether we can afford to live without the reassurance, comfort, and hard work they are invoked to provide. If such persons did not exist, it seems there would be much motivation to create them and maintain their presence among us.

Listening Beyond Appearances

Moving away from appearances and expectations about "strong Black women" to what Black women say for and about themselves can bring a markedly different image of strength to the fore. Crystal[2] is a thirty-six-year-old, fashionably dressed, attractive mother of two school-age sons. Pursuing her undergraduate degree at an urban university, she in many ways is a strong Black woman—a single parent devoted to her children and working to provide a more secure existence for her family. In my interview with her, I am struck by her forthcoming manner as we talk about her experiences of womanhood: She appears certain in her views and comfortable with herself.

However, when I ask her directly about the concept of "the strong Black woman," what it means to her, and how she has encountered it in her life, I become aware of an underground that is rarely allowed to surface.

> And a lot of people tell me that [I'm strong]. Like when my mom passed, I didn't cry [voice quivering]. And, one of my brothers said that, "I've never seen her cry." . . . I lost my husband . . . . Well, it's been ten years ago. I haven't been married [since]. And my mom said that she was worried about me at first, but she see I'm doing fine. And I noticed my family would, when he first passed, they would be looking at me and . . . I'd turn around and say, "What are you lookin' at me for?" [said quickly in a high-pitched, exasperated voice]. You know, everybody's trying to figure me out. . . . And maybe they think that I'm keeping everything under control, so I'm a strong person, despite *whatever.* [3] Even though deep down inside, you don't be feeling that way. You be feeling like life is just *biting you up* or something

Through inflections in her voice and the tears she begins to shed, Crystal expresses a range of emotions that she does not characteristically reveal, even to family: deep sadness over the passing of her mother, continued grief over the loss of her husband, and frustration over the ongoing difficulties in her life.

Crystal also refers to a "deep down inside." In this space carefully guarded from view, Crystal records recurring instances in which she has needed but failed to receive support and encouragement: "Sometimes, I want to be like, you know, patted on the shoulder or something. . . . Sometimes, I'll be like, 'Damn, my life is not so great. I'm having a hard time. . . .'" From this hidden vantage point, she narrates a counter to strength and provides a commentary on the costs of adhering to the mandate that as a Black woman, "I can handle anything." Feeling and needing more than a "strong Black woman" should, Crystal must contain what she is not permitted to reveal.

Despite thwarting her desires to be assisted and nurtured, appearing strong is critically important to Crystal. Her self-presentation as a "strong Black woman" is a well-practiced strategy for personal esteem and protection.

> I hide my emotions a lot. So I think when people *see* you doing good from outside, they think you're a strong person. . . . I think I *like* the idea when people see me as a strong person, and not a weak person. I don't know why. It just makes me feel good. It's, it's crazy. . . . Because it's like, I *want* people to look at me as a person that I *know* I can go to Crystal and get what I want, but at the same time, I really want them to leave me the hell alone. So I don't know. You know, it's like, I don't want them to say, "Well, I know she doesn't have it." I want them to know, "Yes, she *does*." But at the same time, I don't want them to ask [chuckle].

Embracing the idea of strength brings Crystal a level of distinction. She becomes a capable person, someone who can reliably provide for others' emotional and financial needs. However, this virtue also leaves her with a set of irreconcilable oppositions out of which she must live her life: She cannot be both strong and have needs of her own; she cannot share what is going on "deep down inside" and retain the esteem of those around her; and she cannot take care of others and expect reciprocation. Such is the dilemma of strength—to choose appearances and remain unknown to other people, or to choose truth and risk being disregarded by them. Crystal selects what many other Black women see as the lesser peril: She invests in the appearance of her invulnerability, other-directedness, and lack of needs, and hopes that despite being taken in by the performance, others will somehow "leave me the hell alone" and not make such demands of her.

Crystal's experiences of being perceived as stronger—that is, more able and less vulnerable—than she is are far from singular. Black women commonly face such expectations and participate in similar mismatches between self-assessments and outward self-presentations. For Crystal, maintaining the illusion of her strength has relational costs, affecting her ability to experience recognition and mutuality among those closest to her. For many other women like Sondra, a married mother in her forties, the costs are embodied and compromise their physical and emotional wellness.

> I just think that, we're always, on the surface saying, "Okay, yup, I'll do it. I'll do it." And then in our rooms by ourselves, we're like, "How the *hell* am I going to do it," you know? But you figure out a way, but then, you don't let those feelings *out* to anybody, so, eventually, it's just a time bomb waiting to go off. So, and the heart attack rate's high in the Black community.

Sondra intimately knows what Black women experience and must manage in their lives precisely because they are perceived as strong. From this knowledge, she also contests prevailing medical views of distresses, such as heart disease, as the consequences of genetics or lifestyle. Rather she insists that a largely normalized and highly problematic social backdrop exists to such health conditions: the compromised and exploitative material and relational life circumstances Black women endure in the name of their strength. Continually agreeing to numerous labor-intensive tasks, having no one in whom to confide, and suppressing emotions of doubt, anger, and frustration are regular dimensions of Black women's experience of strength. And, like Crystal, Sondra distinguishes between "surface" behavior to appear strong, and what happens out of sight, "in our rooms by ourselves." Such a split in consciousness reflects the extensive accommodations utilized by Black women to prevent discrepant emotions from becoming evident. However, in the process of keeping up the appearance of strength, Black women's bodies become repositories for the thoughts, feelings, and realities that contradict the one-dimensional view of them as unflaggingly capable and ever resilient.

As Crystal and Sondra describe, the word *strength* is both a social expectation and a personal strategy. As a demand, strength requires that Black women act as if they were invulnerable to abuse; and in adopting strength as a self-protective strategy, Black women present themselves as capable of weathering all manner of adversity. In other words, many Black women fight strength with strength: They manage unfair claims as though such were legitimate. However, on the other side of such categorical expectations are enforced silences. Invocations and practices of strength overlook the fact that Black women are subordinated within race, class, and gender hierarchies; that abuses both material and relational occur given such entrenched structural imbalances in power; and that many Black women respond to such duress through their bodies.

A Voice-Centered Framework

Oppression within the United States is not only a material reality, but a psychologically invasive practice. Subordinated groups are encouraged to embrace social lies as their own reality—that is, to "become wedded to what within ourselves we know is a false story" (Gilligan 2006, 59). Such lies or discourses are frameworks of beliefs generated by those with the power to define reality for others. As hegemonic tools, they are used to infuse psyches and social practices with particular meanings directed toward the legitimation of an unjust social order. Such commonsense ideas attempt to secure individuals' active consent by encouraging them to deem noncompliant views—their "deep down inside[s]"—as deviant, unreliable, and therefore discreditable. However, as a growing body of research reveals, the psyche—or what post-structuralists refer to as our subjectivity—is capable of being a resistant space.

Despite the existence of discourses and social pressure to conform to the identities and beliefs that inhere in them, we are not fully determined by those expectations. As post-structuralist scholar Chris Weedon ([1989]1997, 109) explains, subjectivity is a contested and vital site for both social control and social transformation.

> Subjectivity works most efficiently for the established hierarchy of power relations in a society when the subject position, which the individual assumes within a particular discourse, is fully identified by the individual with her interests. Where there is a space between the position of subject offered by a discourse and individual interest, a resistance to that subject position is produced. . . . The discursive constitution of subjects, both compliant and resistant, is part of a wider social play for power.

Our subjectivity contains multiple, shifting, and contradictory stances for several reasons. Conflicts between what we should do according to these varied discourses can engage our cognitive ability to wonder about possible options. Furthermore, our lived experiences offer us opportunities for building knowledge from the ground up and not only from the imposition of discourse-driven order. Thus, included in our psyches is the presence of widely accepted points of view that places us in good stead with others, as well as our individual attempts at meaning-making that fail to fall neatly within such conventions. Importantly, then, our subjectivity both conforms to as well as challenges the parameters set by our social settings.

Language is a critical venue for the empirical exploration of subjectivity. "Voices" or ways of meaning-making are identifiable by the degree to which they carry forward conventional beliefs or discourses.[4] Voice-centered (rather than discourse-focused) research highlights the complexity of subjectivity. Attending to the overlooked and distorted experiences of women, voice-centered inquiry has sought to access and understand a central dynamic: the distinctions between cultural understandings of women or how they are *supposed* to think, feel, and act, and the perspectives or voices of individual women that are relatively "free from second thoughts and instant revision" (Gilligan 2003, 25). As Dorothy Smith (1987, 107) argues, to focus on women's voices rather than prevailing social discourses is a subversive act of "creat[ing] the space for an absent subject." It is also an intentional attempt to access the "subjugated knowledge" (Hill Collins 2000, 251) that oppressed groups and individuals create in order to sustain themselves in situations of inequity.

Drawing on her work with teenage girls, Lyn Mikel Brown (1998, 36) describes how thought and behavior, while strongly patterned by discourses, are not fixed:

> [The girls] struggle with, critique, and resist what passes as feminine expression and behavior, *even as* they come to speak through culturally sanctioned, patriarchal voices of femininity, and publicly perform, at times even judge other girls, along the same narrow standards.

Listening to such girls over time and carefully examining their talk reveals a general principle. In the face of multiple social discourses, we can feel and speak consent. We can also engage in surface conformity, consciously "ventriloquating" (Brown 1998) words and performing actions of acceptability. Lastly, we can outwardly resist expectations. In other words, speech and behavior have the potential to reflect as well as critique and undermine "the hegemony of various available and ideological points of view, approaches, directions, and values" (Brown 1998, 106). Consequently,

attention to both voices and discourses in the speech of interviewees places in relief ongoing and disputed processes of social
control. Such critical activity, however, can escape scrutiny when
the investigative focus is only on behavior or when speech is interpreted as though it were the carrier of flat, self-evident utterances.
Furthermore, by attending to the meaning-making of individuals,
voice-centeredness retains a sensitivity to the diversity of responses
evident as people engage with the discourses and material conditions of disenfranchisement.

The Listening Guide

Out of voice-centered concerns regarding how subordination impacts the subjectivity of women has emerged a particular empirical tool, the Listening Guide.[5] Described as a simultaneously feminist, literary, and clinical method (Brown and Gilligan 1992), the
Listening Guide conceives of the interview situation as an opportunity to elicit multilayered texts of human social experience.
As Lyn Mikel Brown and Carol Gilligan (1992, 23–24) summarize
from their development and use of the Guide to study the adolescent experiences of girls:

> Our Listener's Guide . . . is responsive to the harmonics of
> psychic life . . . the polyphonic nature of any utterance,
> and the symbolic nature not only of what is said but also
> what is *not* said. We know that women, in particular, of-
> ten speak in indirect discourse, in voices deeply encoded,
> deliberately or unwittingly opaque. . . . Therefore, our Lis-
> tener's Guide—as well as being a relational method, re-
> sponsive to different voices—is also a feminist method,
> concerned particularly with the reality of men's power at
> this time in history and its effects on girls and women as
> speakers and listeners, as knowers and actors in the
> world.

The Guide regards speech as a unique portal into an individual's participation in social processes. As such, it carefully examines the thoughts people convey, the manner through which they express these views, and the often layered and contradictory meanings involved in their accounts of social reality. The Guide listens for, but more importantly, *past* social discourses to access a distinction that people often make to themselves—between what they "think" as opposed to what they "*really* think" (Gilligan 1990, 4). Thus, use of the Guide approaches interviewees' utterances as texts with both manifest and more latent content, the latter often existing beyond the sanction of cultural prescription (Anderson and Crowley Jack 1991). And it is the interviewer's responsibility to listen for such undertones in speech.

The Listening Guide focuses on the less evident and often more socially disapproved aspects of speech, "the coded or indirect language of girls and women, especially regarding topics . . . that [they] are not supposed to speak of" (Tolman 1994, 326). During the interview sessions, it directs researchers to adopt a stance of nonjudgmental responsiveness toward the words of the other person. Throughout analysis, it insists on multiple readings of interview text focused on different aspects of the psyche—social discourses, references to self, and distinct forms of meaning-making in the face of such discourses. Because it draws explicit attention to the psyche's layered constitution through discourses and voices, the Guide makes evident the assemblage of conforming and transgressive thoughts and behaviors that constitute a person's subjectivity (Gilligan et al. 2003).

A Voice-Centered Project: Rationale and Methods

At its core, *Behind the Mask of the Strong Black Woman: Voice and the Embodiment of a Costly Performance* is the product of listening. Because of the utility of strength claims to a range of race-gender groups seeking to avoid a confrontation with oppressive realities, assertions and images about Black women need not be truthful ones. In order to move beyond such myth-making to an examination of lived realities, *Behind the Mask* focuses on the voices of fifty-eight Black women, and their discussions of what strength means to them. It traces how a discourse of strength has been constructed in society, and how as a strategy of womanhood it is introduced to Black girls through their mothers and women kin. *Behind the Mask* investigates how both the expectations and the strategy of strength envelope Black women in silence, stoicism, and ongoing struggle, and how maintaining these processes impacts them body and mind.

In the five-year period of 2001–2006, I engaged in an exploratory study of Black womanhood.[6] I recruited participants through flyers, social and professional networks, and word-of-mouth. The women who spoke with me included nontraditional college students enrolled in an open-admissions university and an urban women's college, members of a loose friendship circle in a government agency, and individuals I encountered in my life as a Black woman and an academic. Whether introduced to the project by posters, key informants, or personal invitation, most of the women predicated their agreement to participate on having knowledge of me. That is, their willingness to reveal aspects of their lives hinged on knowing who I was—that I was an acquaintance of someone they trusted, a professor they had heard about, someone they had met personally, or that I, too, was a Black woman.

Within the interviews, many women stated that the opportunity to focus on their womanhood was generally a novel and fruitful experience, one which they described as cathartic. Given the documented unease of Black women with questioning their strength or having challenged this seemingly unassailable aspect of their personhood (Boyd 1998; Dorsey 2002; hooks 1993; Shorter-Gooden and Washington 1996), I sought to create a responsive interview space in which they could speak about aspects of what they knew and experienced without feeling judged as less than strong or other than authentically Black. This approach reflected my desire to have conversations about strength—not as an identity or essential core that defined Black women, but as a framework they encountered, accommodated to, and sometimes resisted.

My interviews with these women were largely individual, but on occasion were undertaken in pairs or small groups. Lasting from thirty minutes to three hours, they varied in terms of length as well as intensity and detail. Adopting the voice-centered feminist practice of seeing the women as my teachers, as those who held the keys to understanding strength, I sought to be a sympathetic witness to their accounts and to listen for multiple standpoints in their narratives of self and society. I opened interviews with a general statement of my concerns about the paucity of research detailing womanhood from the perspectives of Black women. I also acknowledged that I was seeking the women's assistance in gaining insight into their lived experiences. Working from qualities and statements about womanhood that the women had recorded on a short demographic form, I asked them to discuss the salience of these ideas to their lives. The majority of interview time was spent asking follow-up questions to acquire a more nuanced sense of how and why they saw womanhood in particular ways. I also sought their viewpoints on two specific areas of concern—the concept of the "strong Black woman" and the presence of overeating and depression among Black women. In both instances, I was frank about my position as a Black woman and researcher who was trying to determine the relevance of these experiences given the absence of substantive attention to them in the social science literature.

The women interviewed ranged in age from 19 to 67, with a mean of 35.6 years. Included in the sample are five women born and raised in the Caribbean, as well as three who had lived on the African continent.[7] With regard to socioeconomic status, most of the women could be usefully classified as "newly middle class"

(Hill 2005). That is, their social mobility was recent and often limited to their current households. Like many other middle-class Blacks, they typically worked in majority-white settings while maintaining deep interpersonal and material ties to working-class family and friends (Cole and Omari 2003). Straddling two cultural and social classes provided them with a particular "outsider-within" (Hill Collins 2000) standpoint that promoted their conceptualization of womanhood in relational rather than absolute terms. As a result, the women's talk of their race, gender, and strength often incorporated their awareness of other constructions of womanhood and were rarely narrow or exclusive discussions of personal experiences. Rather, the women regularly articulated points of convergence and difference between their lives and those of the women with whom they interacted at home, in communities, and at work, and brought to the project a wider context of femininities than might be suggested by their age, race, or class status.

That two-thirds of the women spoke about, through, and most often in conflict with a strength discourse suggests its prominence in, as well as its impact on, their lives. And in the first half of this book, it is their voices that carry the arguments I make about strength. That for the remaining one-third of the women the idea of strength seemed to be an echo of a past or distant expectation, relevant to other women but not applicable to themselves in their current positions and contexts, points to the wrongfulness of using strength as a master template for perceiving and measuring all Black women. It is these women's experiences, as well as the critiques that the others make about the accuracy of strength as an account of their womanhood, that motivate my efforts not only to document strength, but to identify some other formulations of Black womanhood. Taken together, the accounts of both groups reveal Black womanhood to be an experience more varied than common representations of "strength" allow.

Using the Listening Guide to focus attention on the contours of the discourse of strength and women's reactions to its imperatives,

I encountered the existence of three voices: accommodation, muted critique, and recognized vulnerability. Associated with their attempts to be regarded as dutiful mothers, partners, and employees, as well as faithful bearers of family traditions, the voice of accommodation reflects Black women's mindfulness of the "shoulds" and "have–tos" in their social worlds. Behavior and thinking are consciously and even willingly altered to conform to the particular expectations impressed upon strong Black women, and to avoid vilification and cultural ostracism as "selfish," "weak," or "white." Evident in Crystal's earlier discussion of strong Black womanhood, her voice of accommodation follows the dictates of strength and draws on the discourse as a reference point for her self-understanding, esteem, and actions.

Although not affecting outward behavior, a second voice of muted critique reflects an unraveling between the discourse of strength and Black women's consciousness. Revealed in talk of spaces akin to Crystal's "deep down inside," this voice privately questions and stands apart from the prescriptions of strength. Women's commitments to the discourse, however, override their growing awareness of the enormous energy involved and costs incurred in appearing strong. As a result, the presence of this voice in their talk rarely interrupts Black women's outward adherence to strength. Nevertheless, by registering the struggles of Black women to keep up the appearance of their strength, the voice of muted critique importantly conveys the existence of often profound, but largely masked, physical and mental distress, including compulsive overeating and depressive episodes.

In contrast to the voices of accommodation and muted critique is the last stance of recognized vulnerability. Through this voice, Black women see and express themselves as multidimensional and developing persons with a variety of human needs and interests. For women speaking in this voice, strength does not exert moral sway over them as a policing regime organizing their perceptions and actions. What the women define as good, important, and valuable are qualities that incorporate varied aspects of their subjectivity and the actual conditions of their lived experiences. Often generated in response to problems of the mind and body that have debilitated a woman, this voice seeks a way of being that does not lead to the erasure and disintegration of self that many come to associate with strength. In the place of being strong, such women commit to the flexibility and vulnerability of being human. Taken together, the presence of these voices reflects the varied and ongoing influences on Black women's thought and behavior, and the challenges they experience to secure self-respect, health, and social acceptance within a stratified society.

A Personal Note on Strength

Although a woman of African descent, I was not raised with the term "strong Black woman." I first encountered the concept in graduate school, when interacting with a fellow Haitian American classmate who was attempting to raise my spirits after a particularly frustrating day of coursework. Her comfort came in the form of reminding me that I was an "SBW," a strong Black woman, and that I could tap into this virtue and reframe my experience. Rather than focus on my hurt, I could envision myself as the descendant of freedom fighters who had made social progress under much more dire circumstances. I could also dismiss the stinging behaviors of some of the white women by characterizing these classmates as whiny, weak, and having been spoiled by their privilege. In doing so, I could trade in "racialized gender" (Nakano Glenn 1992), following strength's commitment to the opposition of race–gender groups to justify a social order riddled with inequities.[8]

Using the term to refer to myself and reinterpret my world did boost my esteem, for a time. But I found placing myself and others in a narrative whose lines were drawn years before in slavery troubling. Outrage over the lack of progress made in social relations seemed muted under an acceptance that racial tensions and culturally specific and mutually exclusive feminine traits still carried the day. And even if this narrative were an accurate one, what was I to do with lingering senses of hurt and vulnerability? What if I didn't always feel strong? Over time, I found that many of my "strong" Black women friends also struggled to name what pained them—rejection from faculty advisors, the insensitivity of class- mates to their particular perspectives on course material, deep wounding by intimate partners, and a general inability of others to see and treat them as human beings. Yet these injuries were routinely concealed by the claim and the expectation that they were "strong enough" to deal with any situation. And I witnessed a disproportionate number of such women stall during parts of the graduate program and in many cases not finish courses of study that they were intellectually very capable of completing. As one told me, unseen by the claim of her strength was that the in- stitution and mistreatment by others had "brought me to my knees."

Since those years, I have come to see strength as a construc- tion of virtuous exceptionality and have puzzled over its origins and effects on Black women. My questioning of strength ties into the indignation I have felt toward the requirement made of people of color and women generally to always rise above the socially orchestrated unfairness placed upon us. As Frank Wu (2003) dis- cusses in his critique of the model minority myth, tales of excep- tionality are duplicitous. Widely disseminated accounts of Asian American success are not a tribute to the abilities and achieve- ments of this culturally and economically diverse group, as much as they are a defense of a racialized and class-stratified social or- der. To the extent that Asian Americans can be touted as able to rise above poverty, language barriers, and exclusion, their "suc- cess" can be used to affirm the justness of American society. In the process, the failures of other "unruly" minorities, namely Na- tive Americans and American-born Blacks and Hispanics, can be expeditiously and seemingly fairly attributed to their own internal or cultural limitations. Because of their ability to deflect attention from a problematic social order, myths about exceptions bolster rather than question entrenched inequitable social relations. These carefully drawn and strategically retold stories of triumph pacify a social conscience that on another level knows that expecting a particular group to always demonstrate its value in terms of superlative achievements is a standard both unnecessary and patently unfair in a democracy. It is at the convergence of expectations of immigrant and Black women's exceptionality that I have come to question under what kinds of social conditions and to what ends exceptionality emerges as a virtue. And as is the focus of this book, I am drawn to explore the real yet often hidden costs these expectations of exceptionality have on those required to be other than human, intrepid and inviolable, and prone to look inward rather than to society to manage social inequity. It is my belief that such exceptions are used to prove rules not of such persons' making and to defend circumstances of dubious benefit to them.

A Road Map

Behind the Mask opens with Chapter 1,"More Than 'the Historical, the Monolithic Me':[9] Deconstructing Strong Black Womanhood." Drawing together Black feminist scholarship in intersectional theory, cultural studies, and women's history, this chapter introduces strength as a strategic discourse that rearticulates long-standing sexist and racist attempts to subordinate Black women. Beginning with Michele Wallace's seminal text, *Black Macho and the Myth of the Superwoman* ([1978]1990), the chapter examines critiques of strength generated by Black feminists over the last thirty years. As discussed in the chapter, Wallace's argument that Black women's actual subjectivity exceeded their characterization as strong opened the doors to an interrogation of strength as a controlling image (Hill Collins 2000) rather than a natural identity. In the process, it allowed important questions to be raised about how expectations of Black women's invulnerability become normalized into strategies of womanhood adopted by individual women, in ways that lend their unwitting support to an oppressive and multiply stratified social order.

Chapter 2,"Living the Lies: Embodying 'Good' Womanhood," draws on an emerging feminist approach to women's distress. Puzzling over the gendering of eating disorders and depressive episodes, this framework suggests that such are physical and emotional expressions of the self-silencing many women undertake to achieve standards of feminine goodness. Drawing connections between this framework and strength, I review a growing autobiographical and clinical literature by Black women experiencing compulsive overeating and depression. I demonstrate how these two distresses reflect an underlying dynamic of denial and the active suppression of strength-discrepant thoughts and realities in the service of maintaining the image of good, that is, "strong" Black womanhood.

Following the theoretical investigations into strength as a discourse of racialized gender and its silencing effects on women's bodies and minds, the next three chapters turn to the interview data. These empirical chapters elaborate a trajectory from normative Black femininity to distress, and from distress toward a wellness grounded in the women's experiential needs. Chapter 3, "Keeping up Appearances: The Performance of Strength," examines the socialization and interactional dynamics that render strength into a centerpiece of Black women's "doing" (West and Zimmerman 1987) of gender. Highlighted are the standards of stoicism, care, and selflessness that Black women encounter from girlhood through adulthood, at home and at work, among intimates and strangers. This chapter also scrutinizes how Black women learn to create and also discredit an internal repository for their vulnerabilities, fears, wants, and angers.

Chapter 4, "Lies Make Us Sick: Embodied Distress Among Strong Black Women," discusses how Black women call upon their minds and bodies to manage prohibited experiences of "weakness" and "inauthenticity." This chapter demonstrates how forms of physical and mental distress—particularly overeating and depressive symptoms and episodes—derive from the proscriptions against "strong" Black women revealing their complexity as human beings. Chapter 5, "Coming to Voice: Transcending Strength," analyzes the social awareness and personal changes that become available to Black women, often in the wake of life-threatening disease or deep emotional harm. When they foreground their actual experiences rather than sociocultural lore about their lives, Black women adopt a strength-critical view of social reality and readily admit their humanity. As a result, they question and resist their characterization as exceptions to the suffering others experience in contexts of oppression. This chapter also explores how such individuals seek alternatives to the examples set by women kin and friends. *Behind the Mask* closes with an epilogue. Entitled "Mules No More, Just 'Levelly Human': A Societal Challenge," this conclusion emphasizes the everyday ways in which people invoke strength and thereby entrench an overarching system of racialized gender. Highlighted is the importance of replacing the lies of strength with an appreciation of Black women as fully human social beings.

1 / More Than "the Historical, the Monolithic Me"

Deconstructing Strong Black Womanhood

> To appreciate the meaning of the symbol—Strong Black Woman—we need know almost nothing of the person.
>
> —Nell Irvin Painter, *Sojourner Truth: A Life, a Symbol*

In the United States, differentiations on the basis of perceived race, socioeconomic status, sexuality, and gender have had a particularly longstanding influence on the life chances of individuals and groups. Historical patterns of domination privilege whites over people of color, men over women, heterosexuals over persons of other sexualities, and the affluent over those without wealth. These oppositions contribute to an overarching "matrix of domination" (Hill Collins 2000) composed of numerous simultaneous and interlocking distinctions. As a result, a few statuses are considered normative and deserving of first-class citizenship, while most others are deemed constitutive of deviance and requiring subordination.

The placement of groups in particular statuses within the matrix of domination is justified through the generation and dissemination of "controlling images" (Hill Collins 2000). As representations of subordinated groups, controlling images guide behavior toward and from these persons, constrain what is seen and believed about them, and when internalized, profoundly influence the self-perceptions of the marginalized. As products of the social organization of power, such images define the parameters of appropriate and transgressive subject positions for a particular group. Thus, pervasive and widely accepted controlling images of people of color, the poor, sexual minorities, and women depict these structurally disempowered groups as childlike, naturally evil, complacent with their subordination, or as having a corrupting influence on civil society. In the process, compulsory heterosexuality, male-centeredness, economic privilege, and whiteness are legitimized as indisputably normative and socially necessary values and qualities.

Like stereotypes, controlling images are generalized representations about a group. However, the concept of controlling images insists upon a further point: these generalizations do not simply emerge from erroneous thinking but are *created* by an oppressive order to police marginalized groups and naturalize their disempowerment. To secure material conditions of subordination, such images draw both power and resistance potential away from oppressed persons. Because controlling images are deployed to bring thought and behavior in accordance with the matrix of domination, to cause people to become "docile bodies" (Foucault 1977) rather than transformative subjects, they provide a "disguise, or mystification, of objective social relations" (Carby 1987, 22). Rendering social injustices into "natural, normal, and inevitable parts of everyday life" (Hill Collins 2000, 69), controlling images are the ideological glue that secures the matrix of domination and its goal of reproducing "rich, white, Christian, male, heterosexual power" (Bem 1995, 46; see also, Connell 1995; Hill Collins 2000; Ridgeway and Correll 2004; Risman 2004).

Understanding Racialized Gender:
An Intersectional Framework

To appreciate these multiple differentiations and divisions constitutive of a matrix of domination, Black feminists, among others,
have developed the concept of "intersectionality" (Combahee
River Collective 1982; Crenshaw 1991; Hill Collins 2000; King
1988). Intersectionality approaches gender (or any other social
division) as articulated through other salient dimensions of difference, such as class and race. With regard to women specifically, intersectionality moves away from a static and generic notion of "femininity" to the recognition of *femininities*, and the
distinct prescriptions and privileges that women are accorded
given their combined race, class, and sexuality statuses (Pyke and
Johnson 2003). It insists that we see the plural and hierarchical
ways in which categories of women are called into being and
given social significance, in relationship not simply to "men" and
"masculinity" but also to each other (Alarcon 1990). As a result,
intersectional analyses can easily grasp as a social fact rather
than a paradox that a white woman of upper-middle class standing experiences limited options compared to those of a man of
the same race and class, while the same woman possesses and
can exert enormously powerful advantages relative to poor white
women and women of color generally. Recognizing a multiplicity
to women's experiences, then, intersectionality cautions against
using any partial formulation of femininity as representative of
all. To engage in such a practice is to erase the significant experiential and material differences among women, and to underplay
the complexity of oppression (Richie 2000). As expressed by the
late writer–activist Audre Lorde (1984, 133), intersectionality's
theoretical and political goals include the understanding that a
woman is "not free while any [other] woman is unfree, even when
her shackles are very different."

An intersectional approach reveals that controlling images of gender have always been racialized in the United States. Consequently, they have reproduced a continuum that opposes constructions of white and Black womanhood as anchoring extremes (Hurtado 1989; Marynick Palmer 1983; Nakano Glenn 1992). Maintaining such a hierarchy of racialized gender within the United States has required the careful imagining and regulation of Black female bodies (Manring 1998), and in this, the discourse of strength has played a foundational role.

Since slavery, who Black women have been imagined to be has buttressed a whole social order built upon their hard work, alterity, and relative powerlessness to be the self-directed center of the organization of power. Explains Michele Wallace ([1978]1990, 107),

> Through the intricate web of mythology which surrounds the black woman, a fundamental image emerges. It is of a woman of inordinate strength, with an ability for tolerating an unusual amount of misery and heavy, distasteful work. This woman does not have the same fears, weaknesses, and insecurities as other women, but believes herself to be and is, in fact, stronger emotionally than most men. Less of a woman in that she is less "feminine" and helpless, she is really more of a woman in that she is the embodiment of Mother Earth, the quintessential mother with infinite sexual, life-giving, and nurturing reserves. In other words, she is a superwoman.

Unlike white conventionally feminine women, who are prized, pedestaled, and able to enjoy race and often class privileges, the strong Black woman is a "female Atlas" (Gillespie [1978]1984, 32), invoked and expected to carry the weight of the world on her sturdy shoulders. With regard to hegemonic gender expectations, she is deemed more capable than all men and less incapable than white women. Characterized as emotionally resilient, physically indomitable, and infinitely maternal, this superwoman is endowed with those very qualities that preclude her exploitation. Because she is not simply a woman or a human being but a "superwoman," she cannot be victimized and therefore does not suffer under her circumstances, no matter how extreme.[1]

The Controlling Image of Strength

Critiques of strength as an ideological construct and a problematic framework have been slow to develop, even among Black feminists, because the idea of "strong Black women" carries much emotional weight. Not only an intelligible and well-received "folk category" among Black women, strength is also a general point of consensus among Americans regarding Black women's distinctiveness (Shambley-Ebron and Boyle 2006, 199). Embraced as a "powerful cultural signifier," strength is viewed as a "link to generations of Black women who have overcome adversity, slavery, and racism" (Edge and Rogers 2005, 22). It is therefore fiercely claimed by Black women, particularly in the face of perceived attempts to erase their cultural and experiential uniqueness through facile and often unfavorable comparisons to white women (Donovan and Williams 2002).

As Sheila Radford-Hill (2002, 1086) describes, a strong Black woman typically learns from women kin to combine "attitude, altitude, image, and faith" so as to develop "a self-concept that [can] withstand the all-too-common experiences of male rejection, economic deprivation, crushing family responsibilities, and countless forms of discrimination." Viewed in this way, strength appears to be a culturally generated measure for protecting Black women against a life structured against them. As a result, it is the term and self-identification that many Black women know and cherish well before and often as a virtuous alternative to what some perceive as a largely self-absorbed hegemonic femininity, even in its feminist articulations (hooks 1984; Lorde 1984). As hip-hop feminist Joan Morgan (1999, 35) writes of her upbringing within a West Indian household, "I did not know that feminism is what you called it when black warrior women moved mountains and walked on water. Growing up in their company, I considered these things ordinary." Determination, caring, the ability to manage adversity, and a defined and resilient sense of self are qualities that Black girls and women see widely exemplified by the women closest to them and which they subsequently value as positive marks of distinction over others, especially white women (Shorter-Gooden and Washington 1996, 470). The posture, which asserts that "we're rough and tough, and we don't take no stuff" (Dorsey 2002, 217), is seen among many African Americans to be an appropriate and honest celebration of the fact that Black women possess "a seemingly irrepressible spirit unbroken by a legacy of oppression, poverty, and rejection" (Harris-Lacewell 2001, 3).

Despite these varied cultural and societal investments in strength claims, over the last thirty years, a few Black feminists have challenged a central assertion of the discourse: that Black women are essentially different from others and devoid of any vulnerability to desperation, hurt, and rage under conditions of oppression. Michele Wallace's seminal and hotly contested assertions in *Black Macho and the Myth of the Superwoman* ([1978]1990) opened the door to a way of thinking by and about Black women that has enabled other scholars to ask what constitutes Black womanhood and by whose criteria. Examining her own resistance to both conventional white femininity and Black feminine "strength," Wallace began the important work of revealing strength to be a presupposition or myth, whose uncritical acceptance as "reality" valorized troubling social conditions as the inescapable yet dignifying fate of Black women.

Debunking Myths, Unraveling Truths

> The existence of a Sojourner Truth or a Harriet Tubman did not mean that black women were superwomen, any more than their counterparts were supermen. For every single slave woman like Harriet Tubman there were twenty who died in childbirth, went mad, or became old by the time they were thirty. It only meant that some unusually talented women had emerged despite a vicious and cruel system of human devastation.
>
> —Michele Wallace, *Black Macho and the Myth of the Superwoman*

In 1978, Black feminist cultural critic Michele Wallace brazenly called into question the controlling image of strength, its historical roots, and in particular, its effects on Black women's minds and bodies. Placing in view the "involuntary conditions" (hooks 1981, 72) of overwork, discontent, and distress she saw characterizing many Black women's lives, Wallace asserted that claims of strength were reductive accounts that neither fairly assessed the enormity of these conditions, nor recognized how displays of strength could and did occur alongside expressions of real vulnerability and harm. Wallace contended that strength was a story about Black women written from the vested interests of whites and Black men, and she insisted that its uncritical acceptance rendered Black women into capable yet ultimately docile bodies. Identifying strength's operation as a discourse in the larger society, in Black communities, and in the psyches of Black women, Wallace's text broadly outlined its disciplinary functions and successes. In the process, Wallace placed in relief the historical and material underpinnings of the credo of strength that a later Black feminist would describe as, "No matter how bad shit gets, handle it alone, quietly, and with dignity" (Morgan 1999, 91).

Rearticulating Mammy:
The Strong Black Woman

The characterization of Black women as exceptional creatures originated during slavery, within a series of racist justifications for their mistreatment. Embodying both the physical and reproductive labor necessary for the success of a white-controlled slave economy, Black women were depicted as less than human, as having a nature consistent with their use as chattel and sexual prey. Such exploitation necessitated the creation of two archetypes of Black womanhood—the Jezebel and the Mammy. Both drew on the white supremacist formulation of Africans as essentially nonhuman and savage.

The representation of Black women as lustful, predatory Jezebels was central to the political economy of slavery. By portraying Black women as victimizers in their own right, imbued with the force of a natural sexuality that could overcome the civilization and restraint duplicitously claimed by white men, the image of Jezebel excused the sexual violations of the slave system. References to Black women as categorically whorish by nature, then, provided white men with an innocence and unquestionable authority with regard to their power over and abuse of Black women (Gray White [1985]1999; Hill Collins 2000; hooks 1981).

The counterpart to Jezebel was Mammy, the contented slave who exhibited effusive gratitude to her white owners. Constructed in the 1830s, Mammy enabled white southern apologists to promote a sentimental view of U.S. social relations under slavery (Gray White [1985]1999). Hardworking, powerless, and committed to white rule, Mammy reflected the only redeeming embodiment of Black womanhood imaginable within the intertwined race, class, and gender distinctions of the "Old South." She was a Black woman who knew her place of servitude and helped to regulate the behavior of other slaves through her discipline and example. Pictured as a stout, dark-skinned, ever-smiling, diligent, and doting being, Mammy has endured as a comforting image of Black womanhood to whites throughout almost two centuries of literary, academic, and entertainment media (Harris 2001; Manring 1998).

Notions of Black women's distinctiveness—whether in the form of the active sexuality or the servile disposition attributed to them—have never existed in a social vacuum. Despite their apparent behavioral and temperamental differences, both the Jezebel and the Mammy were foils to the white lady, a paragon of female beauty, virtue, and leisure. Furthermore, Black women's physical characteristics were read as robust rather than fragile, and thus as markers of their natural proclivity for sexual activity and heavy labor. Such work served the practical and ideological needs of white slaveholders, both male and female. Archetypes of Black women also contributed to the ideation of particular Black male gender expectations. As the good male slave, the tractable Uncle Tom was Mammy's counterpart, and both were set apart from the sexuality and violence attributed to the troublesome Black Buck and the Jezebel (Hill Collins 2005). Woven into a cultural fiction, these images presented the restriction of white women to the male-defined domestic sphere, and Black men and women to a white-controlled caste as functional, redemptive actions essential for the productivity and stability of society (Gray White [1985]1999).[2]

As bad Black womanhood has increasingly been confounded with the social conditions and bodies of poor women, the image of good Black womanhood has been modernized to represent middle-class respectability in the eyes of whites and Blacks. Although no longer limited to domestic service, employed Black women too often are treated as modern-day mammies (Hill Collins 2005), prized for their fortitude, caring, selflessness, and seeming acceptance of their subordination. Like their historical counterparts, contemporary mammies are quintessentially beings designed to invisibly and uncomplainingly support a social order that regards them as an exploitable source of labor. As a result, "mammification" (Omolade 1994) refers to the interactional dynamics that pressure Black women to assume a status-reassuring deference to whites, particularly in workplaces. Very intentionally, mammification invokes the long history of racialized and gendered comfort imagined in the person of large, African-featured Black women (Harris 2001). Explains bell hooks (1991, 154),

> [R]acist and sexist assumptions that Black women are somehow "innately" more capable of caring for others continues to permeate cultural thinking about Black female roles. As a consequence, Black women in all walks of life, from corporate professionals and university professors to service workers, complain that colleagues, co-workers, supervisors, etc. ask them to assume multi-purpose caretaker roles, be their guidance counselors, nannies, therapists, priests; i.e., to be that all-nurturing "breast"—to be the mammy.

Such "emotion work" (Russell Hochschild 1979) is an unwritten job expectation that neither advances such women nor garners them financial remuneration.[3] Although workplace mammies are regarded as "essential to the functioning of the operation," they are placed in positions of relative powerlessness (Omolade 1994, 56) and assigned tasks largely determined by others. Pressed to become peacemakers and go-betweens for different status groups, a mammy must variously "represent, defend, counsel, and console both her superiors and those who work under her" (Omolade 1994, 56; see also, Grant 1994). Her strength is measured by her ability to meet these demands and to do so without complaint and disruption of the workplace's power dynamics. Such a formulation of their goodness results in Black women being expected to commit to a "lifetime of faithful service that can border on exploitation" (Hill Collins 2005, 145).

Superstrong Mothers: The Patriarchal Investment in Strength

Although cross-race interactions can problematically expect strength in Black women to justify their devaluation, the exaction of Black women's labor also implicates their own communities. Particularly salient is the invocation of strength in the service of Black male rule in families and institutions. Michele Wallace's own critiques were strongly motivated by her desire to refute the charge of matriarchy that had raced through the Black community and the larger society in the wake of Daniel Patrick Moynihan's polemic, *The Negro Family: The Case for National Action* (1965). Forwarding a view of Black families as disorganized, entangled in a crippling poverty, and subject to deviant gender norms, Moynihan gave life to the controlling image of Black women as matriarchs, women who undermined the integrity of normatively patriarchal families. Although structurally relegated to the most menial of jobs, low-income Black women were portrayed as compromising the emotional development of Black men and children over and above the influence of long-standing exploitative economic policies and a sluggish move away from a legally segregated state.

Moynihan's assertion of a patriarchal model of family order resonated deeply within both white and Black communities. Identifying a "crisis in Black manhood," the report largely validated a male-centeredness among African Americans that had long posited the necessity of women to be "patient, faithful wives and good, self-sacrificing mothers" (Richardson 2003, 72) in order to establish Blacks as morally fit for full citizenship. Additionally, Black nationalist movements throughout the twentieth century typically forwarded a "virile masculinity" whose only complement was a hardworking yet ultimately compliant womanhood (Gray White 1999, 124).

As many Black feminists charge, a "pervasive 'gender silence'" exists in the Black community, and it particularly shrouds the image of the strong mother (Jones and Shorter-Gooden 2003, 39; see also, Hill Collins 1998). Expected to engage in "selfless acts of love and protection" (Thompkins 2004, 4), such mothers are believed to have an "innate capacity for mothering work," rendering it "natural and intrinsically gratifying" under all circumstances (Hill 2005, 123). The claim of epic maternalism by and about such women who make "a way outa no way" (Jordan [1983]2000) for the benefit and care of their loved ones strategically fails to tell the whole story of their experiences of womanhood.[4] Given this construction of motherhood, Black women who embrace this role are also hampered in their ability to see and contest inequitable care responsibilities, lack of reciprocity in relationships, and abuses suffered. In this way, invoking Black women's strength can be a strategy for normalizing sexist impulses within their communities.

Wallace ([1978]1990, 108–109) provides a vivid example of this patriarchal ploy. She recounts watching a news story about an impoverished Black woman surrounded by "numerous small, poorly clothed children," the family living in a seemingly "rat-infested, cramped, and dirty" apartment lacking heat and hot water. Although the overwhelmed woman was in need of various forms of support—financial, emotional, and physical—Wallace's companion, a doctorate-holding director of an outpatient clinic, has a curious yet telling reaction:

> My friend, a solid member of the middle class now but surely no stranger to poverty in his childhood, felt obliged to comment—in order to assuage his guilt, I can think of no other reason—"That's a *strong* sister," as he bowed his head in reverence.

Taken aback by what strikes her as a callous response to obvious human misery, Wallace finds his use of the word "strong" both insincere and strategic. The "reverence" it expresses is essentially a shallow cover for its utility: to minimize outrage about this wom-an's circumstances, to render unnecessary any assistance to her, and to enable an onlooker to conveniently and expeditiously dis-charge any feelings of responsibility or "guilt." Furthermore, his invocation precludes any examination of the woman's situation: it does not uphold an expectation of paternal responsibility, it fails to consider the conditions under which the children were con-ceived (by choice or under duress), and it does not ask whether, as a poor woman, she had access to alternatives to motherhood as a marker of social maturity and value. Instead, the appeal to the discourse denies the relevance of such questions by ascribing to her and other Black women in similar disparaging circumstances a singular imperviousness to injustice and harm.

Further examining assertions and deployments of strength claims within Black communities, Marcia Ann Gillespie illustrates their utility to normalize sexist constructions of social life. As the "ultimate heroine" of her community, a strong Black woman is a maternal figure expected to "accept the assumption that women's work is never done . . . [because] she's only too willing to let others add to the pile" ([1978]1984, 33). Gillespie places an unflinching light on the systematic and culturally approved abuses of Black women's concern for others and their hard work.

> Think about it: how many times have you heard the term applied to a woman whose life no rational person would choose in a million years? Some sister, struggling under an impossible load, who'd love to be able to shrug her shoul-ders or at least have a few other shoulders to share the burden with. "That's a strong Black woman," someone will say in a solemn, near-reverent tone that is usually followed by a moment of silence. It's almost as if one were judging a performance instead of empathizing with her life. As a re-sult, her complexities, pain and struggle are somehow made mythic. . . . (33)

As Gillespie contends, such women are reduced to a less than human status because they are rendered into spectacles. "Placed on a pedestal to be admired rather than helped," strong Black women become virtuous figures to be judged or emulated, but they are not seen sympathetically as persons to be assisted, understood, or protected (Gillespie [1978]1984, 33).

None of the social distance effected by race, class, and gender divisions is questioned or overcome through appeals to Black women's strength. In fact, because these pedestals are the base that supports the efforts and needs of others, a Black woman's movement from this narrow place of worship threatens the stability of the matrix of domination. As a result, Gillespie ([1978]1984, 33) implicates strength in Black women's devaluation:

> Of course she [the strong Black woman] is a person fashioned by the patriarchy; the rules were imposed on her as part and parcel of the tradition and women were trained to pass it on. Sacrifice, hard work and silence are part of our heritage.... Even today when we extol the virtues of our mamas, most often it's a litany of hard work, of what she did without and what she gave—never what she took or expected or demanded as her due.

Assuming their place on this glorified pedestal of strength silences much of Black women's ambivalence toward "being unappreciated and devalued" as mothers, caretakers, and problem solvers in their communities (Gray White 1999, 90). Enduring ongoing shifts of paid work, childrearing, and extended family support, such women have not been protected from relational and sexual exploitation. Furthermore, Black women's strength has too often and too easily been called upon to compensate for the lack of men's accountability to the women and children in their lives (Hill Collins 2000, 174). As a result, many Black women have had to "'assume the position' of abuse" and "absorb mistreatment" within families and community institutions as a "measure of [their] strength" (Hill Collins 2005, 227).

Remaining on the pedestal of their strength has also required Black women to make a critical concession: They have been expected to place a commitment to the race, as defined by men focused solely on their own enfranchisement, over attention to gender, which is often viewed by those men as a divisive, private matter (Combahee River Collective 1982; Hill Collins 2005; Sizemore 1973). The valorizing of Black men's oppression in the larger society has problematically limited attention to the combined realities of racism and sexism that Black women experience. Consequently, speaking up about strength, particularly through its manifestation in Black motherhood, challenges patriarchal expectations of Black women's unquestioned exhibition of a male-centered racial solidarity.

To scrutinize the family and care responsibilities placed upon Black women is not to undermine or devalue such work that has been community-building and resistance-sustaining. Rather, such examination raises questions about how these loads become restricted exclusively to the bodies of Black women. Doing so enables an investigation of the ways in which claims of their heroic motherhood have been used to render commonplace a level of self-sacrifice that many Black women have found difficult to critique let alone escape (Hill Collins 2005). As Kariamu Welsh (1979, 39) shrewdly argues in the popular women's magazine *Essence*, too often claims of Black women's strength displace recognition of their humanity and the violations they experience within their families and communities: "I am not *that* strong that I should endure rape, beatings and other abuses and then sit in a rocking chair, pick out my favorite spiritual and prepare to bear another child.... [N]othing intrinsic in our nature requires us to suffer.... I'm strong enough to be human, no more and no less." Such "selfless maternal giving is a sign of neither self-love nor strength" argues bell hooks (2001, 39), but rather is a marker of how actively the humanity, complexity, and agency of Black women is denied, under appeals to their exceptional strength.

Strength and the Subjectivity of Black Women

> [The Strong Black Woman] is a larger than life mannequin, a stiff unyielding figure erected to fend off external critique and shield internal pain and sorrow. The Strong Black Woman is a reactionary being who grows out of the fears and very real dangers that confront black women on a daily basis, and her presence is often an obstacle to the self-reflection and growth necessary to create change.
>
> —Allison Dorsey, "White girls" and "Strong Black women"

As an articulation of racist and sexist interests, the discourse of strength is deployed to render Black women into self-disciplining bodies who uphold the social order. The success of the discourse becomes evident not when it is experienced by Black women as a set of expectations and practices imposed on them, but when it effortlessly shapes their thinking and behavior "from the inside" (Martin 2003, 57), dangerously blurring boundaries between oppression and affirming self-expression.

In her original work on the myth of the superwoman, Wallace paints a very bleak picture of the subjectivity of Black women and girls under the material and ideological conditions of strength. During her own involuntary, month-long stay in a home for runaway teenagers, Wallace observed the male-identification, poverty, abuse, and lack of legal standing all impinging on the existence of low-income Black and Hispanic adolescent girls. Drawing on this experiential knowledge, Wallace ([1978]1990, 108) later challenged the matriarchy-minded with descriptions of what such girl–women actually face and concede to in their environments.

> Now I want you to picture a little black girl in a jungle that has no tigers and lions, but poverty, ignorance, welfare centers, tenements, rats, roaches, inadequate schools, malevolent teachers, pimps, Forty-second Streets, Eighth Avenues,

heroin, hypodermic needles and methadone, opportunis-
tic preachers and community leaders, a narrow range of
career possibilities, always impending pregnancies, steril-
ization, poor medical services, corrupt lawyers, an insensitive and illogical court system, and two races of men who
prey upon her as a sexual chattel and a beast of burden.
And suppose that behind this black girl, there was a whole
string of little black girls who had faced this same jungle
with their imaginary advantages and been defeated. Would
it not be an act of unkindness, of extreme injustice really,
to tell her that she was a woman of special strengths, of exceptional opportunities?

Without white-, male-, or class-privileged status, Wallace insists
that poor Black girls and women are afforded virtually no protec-
tions and recognitions as "inherently valuable" human beings
with "the right to search for happiness and freedom (Smith 1998,
33). The devaluation of such women is evident in the lack of outrage over their mistreatment and their continued misrepresenta-
tion as other than sympathetic, multidimensional figures.[5]

Struck by incongruities between the reality and representation
of Black female adolescence, Wallace proposes that there is no de-
fensible way of asserting that such a girl has a privileged status and
enviable prospects for her development. She concludes that invocations of strength inhere to a discourse meant to deceive and dis-
empower, and that tragically, Black girls and women taken in by
the discourse become disconnected from their violations, vulnerabilities, and the overall costs and conditions of their much prized
survival ([1978]1990, 108). Furthermore, Wallace critiques Black
women's self-presentation as a "survival strategy" (Ward 2000) that
inures them to a dangerous cycle of wounding, isolation, and denial. As a result, such girls and women become docile bodies (Foucault 1977), crafted out of the subordination they come to see as
their birthright.

Wallace names this gross deception "the myth of the super-woman," and charges it with systematically overlooking Black women's entrapment and experiences of mental and physical distress. In its wake, frustrations, fears, and harm become what large numbers of Black women dismiss as unremarkable aspects of their existence. Explains Wallace ([1978]1990, 105–106),

> And she need not end up in "trouble" necessarily, in prison, in a juvenile home, on drugs, on the streets as a prostitute, or having a baby at fourteen, but just in a dead-end job that she hates, in an unhappy destructive marriage, having children she doesn't want, or wasn't ready to have, or shouldn't have had. Or she might just become a quiet alcoholic, overweight and with high blood pressure, or chronically depressed. The point is that the life of such a young woman is gone and she never once exercised any control over it.

Wallace insists that such abuses and limitations are routinely suffered by Black girls and women but are also consistently minimized by appeals to their strength, their presumed power to defy victimization.

A Subjectivity in Excess of Strength?

Although passionately describing how strength compromises Black women's emotional, physical, and relational wellness, Wallace presents Black girls and women as having a subjectivity largely dominated by the discourse. In the process, she leaves little room to understand the possibility of resistance, including her own, to this mandate. However, other Black feminists maintain that while not outwardly contesting their strength, Black women demonstrate a much more complex relationship to this overarching discourse of feminine goodness.

Historian Darlene Clark Hine's (1989) concept of dissemblance attributes more agency to Black women than Wallace concedes. From her examinations of the lives of southern Black women migrants during the early twentieth century, Clark Hine maintains that their bold decisions to flee the South and pursue opportunities northward were often accompanied by an intentional hiding of fears and vulnerabilities. Understood as a general strategy of the oppressed, the concept of dissemblance suggests that the subjectivity of Black women is not reducible to and cannot be directly inferred from their outwardly conforming behaviors.

As a form of managing multiple realities, dissemblance has affinities with W.E.B. DuBois' (1903) oft-quoted concept of double consciousness. However, it offers an interesting twist. Portraying racist oppression as a veil, Du Bois maintained that African Americans were effectively and infuriatingly removed from the fully enfranchised life they could see around them. In contrast, Clark Hine's (1989, 915, 916) use of dissemblance focuses on the agency of individual Black women to effect a "self-imposed invisibility," as they intentionally veiled themselves to protect aspirations and feelings that could easily be shattered by members of white society, and by Black men.

> A secret, undisclosed persona allowed the individual Black woman to function, to work effectively as a domestic in white households, to bear and rear children, to endure the frustration-born violence of frequently under- or unemployed mates, to support churches, to found institutions, and to engage in social service activities, all while living within a clearly hostile white, patriarchal, middle-class America.

Dissemblance is a strategy Black women adopted *both* in the exploitative situations forced upon them (such as their relegation to demanding, low-paying domestic work until well into the twentieth century) as well as in the normative and culturally valued caregiving contexts of family and community life. Clark Hine therefore posits that the threats to Black women's integrity traversed the boundaries of paid and unpaid labor, and of white- and black-dominated living and work spaces. Such pervasive needs for the use of dissemblance reveal that there were very few circumstances in which Black women could be forthcoming about their lives and certain that their realities and aspirations for freedom would not be used against them or employed to advance the interests of others. Thus, Black women's ability to manage what were extensive demands placed upon them by both a white-dominated society and a patriarchal Black community necessitated the creation and careful protection of an inner life from the majority of their daily responsibilities and interactions.

Investigations into the lives of contemporary Black women point to the continuing importance of dissemblance. Writer Charisse Jones and psychologist Kumea Shorter-Gooden (2003) introduce the term "shifting" to name Black women's strategic acts of self-presentation. "[T]o counter the myths and manage direct acts of discrimination," Black women "endlessly compromise themselves to put other people at ease, counteract the misperceptions and stereotypes, and deflect the impact of those hostilities on their lives and the lives of their mates and children" (2003, 4, 63). Despite its origins as a voluntary act or at least an intentional tool of impression management, long term "shifting" erodes a woman's voice and leaves her subjectivity largely dictated by discourses of goodness. As one interviewee in Jones and Shorter-Gooden's study reveals:

> You feel like you gotta be perfect. You gotta be fit. You gotta be smart. You gotta be strong, but not so strong that you offend everybody. You gotta be outspoken, but not too outspoken. You gotta be all these different things. You've got to be able to take crap from people and bite your tongue. . . . You feel that almost every day. (2003, 15)

Shifting is an exhausting use of dissemblance. Reflecting a continuous need to assess what can be divulged to others, the process of shifting reminds us of Black women's constant awareness of how their standing with others is rarely secure or under their ultimate control.

The view of dissemblance and shifting as volitional and effectively self-protective acts is similarly questioned by sociologist Kesho Scott. In her examination of the survival strategies employed by Black women during their lives, Scott concludes that such tactics have attained the status of "unexamined and unquestioned [cultural] traditions" (1991, 8). As Black women conceive of themselves as lone "warriors" charged with maintaining families and communities, the prescription to be strong necessitates the defensive denial of pain, vulnerability, and suffering. "Feeling responsible for everyone" while believing they can "never let down our guard (even to ourselves)," Black women can experience and normalize a level of exhaustion leaving them "already worn out at [age] thirty-five" (1991, 231, 11, 173). This imperative to be strong endures in part because women tell half-truths about "the glory of their own survival" while "cover[ing] up the pain" (1991, 174). Scott contends that as a response to adversity and limited opportunities for protection and validation, strength currently operates as a "habit" among Black women, and thus impedes their well-being. "[N]ot our true birthright," observes Scott (1991, 228), ongoing dissemblance is "a slow death sentence from within."

Taken together, these historical analyses and contemporary psychological explorations suggest that the discourse of strength extorts much from Black women. Whether fostering a self-protective culture of dissemblance or the automatic use of habits of survival, living under the controlling image of strength compromises Black women's psyches and bodies, and undermines their overall agency. Contradicting the common perception that strength sustains Black women and promotes their independence, these concepts describe how Black women pay a high price for appearing strong. Like the "mystique" (Friedan [1963]1983) of ultrafemininity (Morton 1991) forced upon white women, the perpetual impression management of dissemblance and shifting and the culturally sanctioned habits of survival generate profound silences in and about Black women's lives. Eliciting Black women's support as good employees, respectable representatives of the race, and dutiful culture bearers and mothers, strength reduces Black women to the confines of a race and gender order grounded in claims of their lesser humanity. As a "technology" (Martin 2003) of racialized gender, then, strength has the dual status of a tool of exploitation and a marker of virtue. It is this double purpose that hampers rather than promotes Black women's social standing and self-knowledge. Poignantly highlighting the duplicity of strength, Joan Morgan summarizes (1999, 104), "Black women are not impervious to pain. We're simply adept at *surviving*. The problem for [strong Black women] is telling the difference."

Conclusion

Examining strength as a discourse that insists on the exceptionality of Black women reveals its curious, counterfactual, and oppressive logic. Taking race, class, and gender domination as givens, the discourse asserts that the intertwined problems that Black women know well—the compromised opportunities occasioned by poverty, male privilege, and the association of Blackness with expendability—are not grounds for social outrage but acceptable tests of individual mettle. The question then turns to whether such women are "strong enough" to endure these hardships, not whether inherent problems exist in the organization of society. Furthermore, as a strategy of gender upheld in Black communities, strength celebrates Black women's heroic actions and deflects attention from their circumstances. In the process, the social interactions and conventions that create the defining struggle and labor in Black women's lives are rendered invisible. Strength, then, is a backward history of Black women, "written after the fact" of their subordination, abandonment, and protective self-silencing (Gilligan 2006, 62). It is a claim of exceptionality that draws on Black women's bodies and minds to defend a flawed social order.

The attribution of strength depicts "strong" Black women as categorically invulnerable to the violence, poverty, and marginality forced upon them. In refuting this skewed ideology, Black feminists make the straightforward yet elusive point that Black women are simply human, but have been forced to live under dehumanizing social conditions, which the discourse asserts they are uniquely qualified to manage. Such a claim discourages scrutiny of and changes in the social conditions faced by Black women. As Michele Wallace (1990, 227) expresses in a later publication, "The problem with the myth of the superwoman as I saw it once, and still see it, was that it seemed designed to cover up an inexorable process of black female disenfranchisement, exploitation, oppression and despair. Even more important than whether the black woman believes the myth . . . is the way the dominant culture perpetuates the myth not in order to celebrate [Black women] but as weapons against them: 'she is already liberated' becomes an excuse for placing her needs last on every shopping list in town."

Emphasizing struggle, caretaking, endurance, and stoicism as distinctive badges of honor, the strength discourse inures a society as well as Black women's communities to their actual vulnerabilities and the enormity of violations they experience. Because of their concerns with "exposing the hypocrisy of the culture, shared by both black men and white men, regarding the image versus the reality of black women," Wallace (1990, 222) and other feminist scholars recognize that strength is a condition of flagrant subordination regardless of claims by Black women or others to the contrary. Pointing out strength's intimate connections to the matrix of domination and its impact on the subjectivities of Black women, Wallace, Gillespie, hooks, and Scott reveal it to be a calculated strategy for disciplining minds and bodies. In the process, they refuse to be complicit in the reviling or empty celebration of Black women as subhuman, superwomen, or categorically "other." Foregrounding Black women's humanity—their experiences of suffering, frustration, and desire—they illuminate the artificial and constraining limits of strength. Thus, rather than accept that vulnerability and frailty are "traits not generally associated with African-American women" (Gray White [1985]1999, 10), such scholars prompt us to ask how Black women come to register and express these very human reactions to duress in their lives.

2 / Living the Lies

Embodying "Good" Womanhood

There oughta be a woman can break
Down, sit down, break down, sit down
Like everybody else call it quits on Mondays
Blues on Tuesdays, sleep until Sunday
Down, sit down, break down, sit down

A way outa no way is flesh outa flesh. . . .

A way outa no way is too much to ask
Too much of a task for any one woman.
　　　　　—June Jordan, *Oughta Be a Woman*

These suprahuman women have been denied
the 'luxuries' of failure, nervous breakdowns,
leisured existences or anything else that
would suggest that they are complex, feeling
human beings.
　　　　　—Trudier Harris, "This disease called strength"

Women are known by their bodies. Although viewed as metonymies for what is "essentially" female, women's bodies are in actuality "achieved" through the ongoing development of culturally appropriate physical, behavioral, and attitudinal markers of racialized gender. The concept of embodiment acknowledges that the purposes and meanings of human bodies are subject to social regulation. Because the body is made an important carrier of social meaning, it is simultaneously "socially constructed, subjectively experienced, and physically material" (Schrock, Reid, and Boyd 2005, 320).

In their varied social and cultural contexts, "good" women are expected to "do" (West and Zimmerman 1987), as opposed to "undo" (Deutsch 2007), their gender. That is, they fit their bodies and accommodate their minds to the prescriptions—both manifest and latent—of controlling images of femininity. Reproduction, the care of others, attention to appearances, scrutiny of the body, and confinement to limited spheres of activity and influence all are uses of the body to distinguish femininity from masculinity, women from men, a subordinated group from one that dominates it.

Although women's bodies are targets for bringing them in accordance with gender mandates (through society's regulations and violence, as well as its surveillance and management), women also enlist their bodies and minds to subvert society's claims on them. The degree to which a woman knows her subjectivity to be in excess of discursive norms creates a critical space for the generation of new meanings and possibilities for her embodiment. A resulting unruliness can take the form of decorating, utilizing, interjecting, and presenting the body in ways that disrupt its comprehensibility and acceptability. Consequently bodies and minds express, record, and at times resist a range of social meanings imputed to them.

Gender Ambivalence and Feminine Distress

Eating problems and depression are two distresses that offer insight into the ongoing embodiment of femininity. As both physical realities and symbolic processes, they can express women's "gender ambivalence" (Perlick and Silverstein 1994). Highlighting femininity as a category of limitation, devaluation, and confinement, the concept of "gender ambivalence" emphasizes the feminist observation that "psychopathologies that develop within a culture, far from being anomalies or aberrations ... [are] characteristic expressions of that culture" (Bordo 1993, 141). Or as Betty Friedan ([1963]1983, 9) asserted with regard to the depression and anxiety among 1950s white suburban women, "the problem that has no name" was woven into the cultural fabric: "I and every other woman I knew had been living a lie, and all the doctors who treated us and the experts who studied us were perpetuating the lie, and our homes and schools and churches and politics and professions were built around that lie."

As technologies of gender (Martin 2003), idealized notions of womanhood must render questionable the existence of real women who are other than the norm of what a good woman is supposed to be, want, know, accept, and do. Consequently, the management of distress enlists much self-surveillance. Focusing on the contemporary controlling image of youthful, slender beauty most directly associated with white, middle-class women, Kim Chernin ([1982]1994, 106) demonstrates its encouragement of self-discipline and denial of social pathologies:

> Consider what it means to persuade a woman who is depressed and sorrowful and disheartened by her entire life, that if only she succeeds in reducing herself, in becoming even less than she already is, she will be acceptable to this culture which cannot tolerate her if she is any larger or more developed than an adolescent girl. The radical protest she might utter, if she correctly understood the source of her despair and depression, has been directed toward herself and away from her culture and society. Now, she will not seek to change her culture so that it might accept her body; instead, she will spend the rest of her life in anguished failure at the effort to change her body so that it will be acceptable to her culture.

Gender ambivalence suggests that although anorectics, over-eaters, bulimics, and depressives recognize, on some level, that a wrong has been done to them, this awareness is often supplanted by internalization, self-doubt, and a renewed commitment to dis-claiming what others refuse to recognize as a problem. The success of such socialization leads women to respond to the eruption of "unfeminine" emotions and desires with increases in self-surveillance (Ussher 2004).[1] An incipient social critique is ren-dered into an individual fault or problem that a woman must manage on her own or express through the mistreatment of her own body. In other words, one fights femininity with femininity, using the disciplinary tools of being a good woman to hold oneself in check when one's excess beyond such expectations becomes evident.[2]

In addition to acknowledging the social causes of these dis-tresses, the concept of gender ambivalence emphasizes that indi-vidual women can and do strike out against imposed forms of femininity. Their resistance draws on experiences, feelings, and thoughts that fall outside the purview of such discourses. Viewing common women's distresses as "embodied *protest*" (emphasis in original), Susan Bordo (1993, 168, 175) argues for the implicit mean-ing of such problems:

> Loss of mobility, loss of voice, inability to leave the home, feeding others while starving oneself, taking up space, and whittling down the space one's body takes up—all have symbolic meaning, all have *political* meaning under the varying rules governing the historical construction of gender. . . . It is as though these bodies are speaking to us of the pathology and violence that lurks just around the corner, waiting at the horizon of "normal" femininity.

Such symptoms are tied to a number of problematic assump-tions evident in the lives of women—that they accept social powerlessness as natural, that they uncomplainingly take on the care and keeping of others as an all-consuming life duty, and that they internalize or keep from view any discontent. The symptoms also reveal how gender is embodied, and how actively notions of femininity draw on the resources of women's bodies and minds. Moreover, these symptoms can reflect social critiques that women may express through their bodies, seeking "disorder" over continued existence as "normal" yet profoundly dissatisfied persons. However, through medicalization and women's learned propensity to see their bodies as unreliable sources of knowledge, such unruliness is often pathologized and stripped of its political potential.

Eating Problems: Responses to Violation

Drawing attention to the intertwined inequalities of race, class, and gender, Becky Thompson (1994, 8, 12) contends that eating is a venue for many women to register and protect themselves from the "socially induced injuries" and "atrocities" visited upon them. She argues that struggles over food, body size, and eating are multifaceted attempts by women to garner security and to exert influence over painful circumstances. They arise in the wake of structural violation—the sexual, physical, and emotional abuse of women; racist attacks on the bodies and minds of women of color; poverty's disempowerment; and the shaming and banishment of lesbians from full citizenship. Consequently, many women may resort to eating patterns—whether overeating, excessive dieting, or purging practices—to shelter themselves from the reality of societal arrangements that mistreat their bodies and deny them even a basic level of security and acceptance in their social worlds.

Thompson's identification of eating problems among women of color as well as white women, lesbians as well as heterosexuals, and the poor as well as the middle class contests discursive attempts evident in medical, epidemiological, and even feminist literatures to limit such distresses to a privileged group and to inscribe their experiences of womanhood as normative. The devaluation of women in the form of violence (actual and threatened), restricted work and life opportunities, and stigmatizing cultural imagery is a pervasive rather than limited backdrop to the genesis and logic of eating problems.

Although eating problems have a material effect on bodies and minds, they are also symbolic illnesses through which violation and social critique are expressed. Respecting the efforts—valiant yet flawed—of women attempting to resist harmful aspects of particular femininities, Thompson's coining and use of the term "eating problem" rather than the more common "eating disorder" serves two purposes. First, the phrase emphasizes the social rather than presumed psychological causes of disordered eating. In the medical literature, this practice has tended to reinscribe particularly white women within a set of stereotypically feminine traits such as malingering and self-absorption. Additionally, while recognizing that eating problems are costly and harmful, the phrase recognizes what is less appreciated—that eating practices can be utilized to find safety and healing in those bodies on which so much violence is inflicted. For many women, like the one quoted below, eating practices are creative and intentional acts of self-protection in the face of trauma, such as childhood sexual abuse.

> I hid my real self inside, very deep inside of a cave or a molecule or a cell. That is where I went. Another part of me that was sort of split off at the same time was the part that you would see.... Eating was the cave, barrier, boundary, safety, and the buffer.... (Thompson 1994, 78)

Beyond the surface manifestations of problem eating exist similar underlying causes, rooted in the material conditions and discursive constructions of women's lives. Thompson (1994, 12) insists, "discomfort with weight, bodies, and appetite are often the metaphors girls and women use to speak about atrocities. To hear only concerns about appearance or gender inequality is to miss the complex origins of eating problems," as well as the resistance to violation embedded in them. As one white bulimic explains, her childhood eating problem began as a response to fraying family bonds, not a desire to be thin: "I think I first threw up in the hope of getting attention.... Things were really bad at my house, as far as my parents fighting. If I could catch their attention that I was throwing up, maybe they wouldn't fight" (Hesse-Biber 1997, 15).

Shifting the focus from individual psyches to social conditions, from sexism to a matrix of domination, Thompson's multiracial feminist approach powerfully challenges a prevailing myopic and hegemonic view of eating disorders: that they are limited to ultrafeminine women who have the luxuries of adequate food and the presumed cognitive sophistication to develop symbolic relationships to their social environments and bodies (Johnson 2005; Thompson 1994, 14). Within Thompson's framework, more significant than the type of eating problem developed is the use of eating to counteract violence, gain security, and create pockets of freedom. Whether engaged in bingeing, purging, or self-starvation, women with eating problems are clamoring for recognition and protection within a society and amidst cultural norms that systematically ignore and dismiss them because they are expendable, because they are "just women" (Orbach [1978]1988; Thompson 1994).

Eating Problems: Not Just for White Girls

Black women can and do imbue their eating with meanings that reflect their own struggles to live with body and mind intact.[3] For reasons I explore, Black women are more likely to register trauma, powerlessness, and gender ambivalence through overeating rather than self-starvation and purging practices (Hesse-Biber 1997; Thompson 1994; Williamson 1998). Like other eating problems, overeating is a "transference process" through which women use their bodies to symbolically absorb and manage injustice in their lives (Thompson 1996). As Sharlene Hesse-Biber (1997, 111) finds, "The intake of large quantities of food in a short time period can serve to numb, soothe, and literally 'shield' (with fat) some women from physical and emotional trauma." For Black women laboring under the burden of strength while immersed in social conditions that assault their minds, bodies, and spirits, bingeing allows them a temporary respite without disturbing their responsibilities to others. Cheaper and with fewer side effects than alcohol, bingeing can provide an overwhelmed mother in poverty with the semblance of safety and self-care, while allowing her to "still get up in the morning, get her children ready for school, and be clearheaded for the college classes she attend[s]" (Thompson 1996, 61). Unrecognized by many, however, is that the costs of such coping are all absorbed and contained within her local body and its deteriorating health status.

Bingeing is a way of registering harm, disappointment, hurt, or outrage. However, this voice of violation is easily overshadowed and discredited by the renewed imposition of the self-silencing and self-policing tools of strength. Such tension is expressed by a college graduate reflecting on her compulsive eating (Johnson 2005, 197):

I was completely unprepared when the job market didn't stand up and take notice of my studies abroad and expensive diploma. Soon I was relying on my mother, stepfather, and boyfriend for financial support. I couldn't even pay my rent.

What I *could* do was eat myself numb. I consumed unspeakable amounts of whatever I could buy in the vicinity of my downtown Brooklyn studio apartment. French fries. Pizza. Macaroni and cheese. Fried whiting sand-wiches shellacked with hot and tartar sauce. Food became a drug I'd use when I was feeling happy, sad, or some-where in between. It was a reward. It was a sedative. Food was my companion.

The "gorging" she describes is purposeful. It is an attempt to man-age a sense of desperation as she encountered a work world resis-tant to her skills and aspirations. This knowledge of what she was doing and why, however, was compromised by the invocation of her invulnerability as a Black woman.

In retrospect, I knew that binging [sic] on a daily basis con-stituted an eating disorder, but I refused to confront it. I was not equipped to deal with that level of reality. We Black women didn't have body image concerns. And even if we did, how could we trouble ourselves with something as frivolous as size when we had racism, AIDS, and a host of other battles to fight? (199)

The discourse of strength actively denies the struggles faced by this woman and reframes her distress as "frivolous" and inauthentic.

The minimizing of her voice—or what she describes as being "not equipped to deal with that level of reality"—is part and parcel of the grooming of girls into "strong Black women." Growing up, they learn that "you're everything to everybody . . . and you don't think about yourself" (Carlisle Duncan and Robinson 2004, 91). As adults, they often look askance at weight management because of their internalization of strength's reasoning that "we have too many other things that we have to worry about," such as shoulder-ing responsibility for the emotional and financial care of families (Walcott-McQuigg et al. 1995, 513). Claiming that Black women have more meaningful battles to fight than weight gain, and insisting that body image concerns are exclusive to "narcissistic, insecure White women without real problems," the strength discourse encourages women to assert that "I'm Black. I can't have an eating disorder" (Johnson 2005, 200). In the process, it silences what this woman knows but is kept from facing: that she is overwhelmed, unhappy, and feels her only recourse is to "numb" herself through binge eating.

In racializing concerns about weight as white and self-indulgent, the discourses of strength and eating problems conspire to induce Black women to move away from an empirical examination of their circumstances. As persons who cannot suffer, strong Black women are denied a vocabulary for examining their overwhelming obligations to others, their limited resources for meeting those demands, and their needs for comfort. While such women may bristle at the scrutiny of their eating, some admit that under these relational and economic conditions, "food [easily becomes] a vehicle that is used to comfort us when we may not have much else" (Walcott-McQuigg et al. 1995, 512). Understood against the backdrop of normative beliefs about strength, steady weight gain experienced by these women suggests that their bodies and eating patterns are not "natural" but reflective of the lack of support and validation they receive as "superwomen."

The painful irony of weight gain is that it, too, is easily subsumed by the strength discourse as a sign of a woman who can "handle the rough times better" (Allan, Mayo, and Michel 1993, 329). Furthermore, cultural norms that value meals as an expression of caring and affiliation, the aesthetic preference for thicker rather than thin figures, a view of dieting and weight-controlling exercise as suspiciously white endeavors (Carlisle Duncan and Robinson 2004; Parker et al. 1995), and beauty ideals more concerned with skin color and hair texture (Leeds 1994; Okazawa-Rey, Robinson, and Ward 1987) than weight collude to make overeating a coping strategy that can evade critique. Whereas clothing and hair are considered important body projects reflecting good grooming, self-pride, and individuality, weight is often framed as a relatively stable and a tacitly distinctive feature of Black women. Thus, the size and shape of a Black woman's body are often interpreted—within Black communities and in the larger society—as symbolic and immutable markers of both her degree of authenticity and her strength. And, because eating is not automatically problematized as it is in white communities, it is a safe strategy for registering discontent. It enables a woman to experience some respite, while not placing her under the direct scrutiny of those who hold her in high esteem for appearing strong. As a result, although "the most respected physical image of black women, within and outside of the community, is that of the large woman," sociologist Cheryl Townsend Gilkes (2001, 183) observes that "some of the most powerless women in the community struggle with overweight and its unhealthy consequences."

Perceived exclusively through "the persistent mammy-brickhouse Black woman image," some women find themselves part of a community of binge eaters. Amidst other large Black girls and women who are similarly "defined as strong and responsible by their peers" (Powers 1989, 134), such women consume food as a direct consequence of the limited access they have to emotional expressiveness and recognition as fully human beings. As one woman laments, "Instead of crying or dealing with our anger, depression and pain, my binge buddies and I laughed . . . suppressing [these emotions] with food" (Powers 1989, 134, 136). Consequently, while making a Black woman appear more racially identified and stronger, weight gain can also mask great devastation and need, and her ambivalence toward being treated as "public property" (Bray 1992, 54).

Despite outwardly conceding to such treatment, strong Black women often develop "conflicted inner visions" (Townsend Gilkes 2001) that arise from the subordination of a voice of vulnerability to the discourse of strength. Speaking of her obesity as the embodiment of the "emotional weight" she carries, Rosemary Bray (1992, 54) explains:

> Black women have assumed so much responsibility in this culture I often wonder how we can still stand up. Who and what supports us? In truth, it is most likely food that sustains us.... We are forever working, loving, volunteering, scolding, nurturing, and organizing—but nearly always for others. And we do all this not because we are stupid or mindless or weak, but because we are human, and because there is no one on the planet who does not want to feel they belong somewhere, even if that somewhere is the wrong place.

"Conflicted inner visions" arise from the mixed societal messages about Bray's value and worth, as well as from her internal struggle to acknowledge a subjectivity that is more complex than that of a "strong Black woman." Having well learned to suppress those voices in conflict with strength, however, many Black women cling to the very identity that is burdening their minds and bodies with excesses of responsibility. Fighting strength with its tools of dissemblance and shifting leads to the continued suppression of realities that, if faced directly, could challenge strength's ideological underpinnings.

Resisting this strategy of strength, Bray correctly concludes that her hunger is a social problem: "And it is gradually becoming clear to me that I am immensely hungry for much more than food. I am hungry for the things all of us are really hungry for: hungry to be truly seen and known, hungry to be accepted the way I am. There may be no more difficult desire for an African-American woman to fulfill" (1992, 90). For these women struggling with overeating, the problem at hand is one of silencing. Perceived as strong Black women, they are actively impeded from recognizing and acting on hurts, disappointments, and fears more easily associated with other race–gender groups. Presenting them as invulnerable to harm, the strength discourse also effects a questionable mind–body split and a division of consciousness. And by subscribing to the discourse, Black women lose direct recourse to what they know, want, and need. As a result, their eating and weight gain become symbolic attempts to acknowledge and speak the vulnerabilities that strength systematically denies.

Policing and Silencing the Self: A Feminist Approach to Depression

A second body problem overwhelmingly affecting women is depression.[4] Although a definitive understanding is still elusive, prevailing medical and lay frameworks posit biochemical roots to the disorder (LaFrance 2007). While not denying an organic contribution to the distress, researchers in what I refer to as "the silencing paradigm" conceptualize it not so much as a unique and pathological state, as portrayed in the medical literature, but as a crisis embedded in the everyday inequitable social relations (interpersonal and structural) that surround and define a woman's existence (Crowley Jack 1991, 1999a; Mauthner 2002; Schreiber 1998, 2001; Schreiber and Hartrick 2002; Stoppard 2000; Stoppard and Gammell 2003).[5] Firmly rooted in qualitative research that seeks to develop richly contextualized understandings of human experience, the silencing paradigm reveals a disconnect between medical etiologies and women's accounts and embodied knowledge of depression. As Rita Schreiber (2001, 96) summarizes, conceptualizing and "treating women's depression without attending to the social forces that promote it can serve to reinforce the status quo by assisting women to adjust to injustice. . . . The individual woman's depression is the end product of a more insidious and prevalent social ill."

Distinctive about work in the silencing paradigm is that inquiry begins from the standpoint of women—that is, the talk and "actualities of people's lives as they experience them" (Smith 1996, 172). Turning to women as guides—in part to remedy the lack of women's perspectives on their distress in the scholarly literature (Schreiber and Hartrick 2002; Stoppard 2000)—the silencing paradigm has generated novel insights into the onset, experience of, and recovery from depression.

Specifically, the silencing paradigm conceives of depression as a psychosocial process in which women lose and then "mourn" a self that has become "submerged, excluded, or weakened" (Crowley Jack 1991, 30) under relationships, identities, and "normative restriction[s]" of feminine goodness (Litton Fox 1977, 805). Such standards are drawn from cultural discourses that, once internalized, exert a moral force that judges and condemns many of the thoughts and feelings that women register as grounded in their actual experiences (Crowley Jack 1999a, 223). The onset of depressive episodes, then, is essentially a period in which women become aware of a longstanding fracture (Schreiber 1998). This disconnect results from doubting and repressing private thoughts that are at odds with the forms of femininity that women are pressured to take on in order to be considered "good" (Crowley Jack 2003). Viewing this socially induced split as the source of women's distress, the silencing paradigm frames the emotional and physical symptoms often associated with depression—feelings of hopelessness and helplessness, the inability to engage in routine activities, social withdrawal, and fatigue—as the embodied manifestation of an underlying erosion of self (Stoppard 2000, 213; see also, Schreiber 2001; Ussher 2004).

Within the silencing paradigm, depression is understood as a complex state of insight and crisis, cognitive awareness and compromised physiological functioning. In their retrospective accounts, women often describe the existence of two distinct selves, one preceding and the other emerging during the depressive episodes. The first is relatively unaware or profoundly afraid of alternatives to feminine goodness in their lives. Although "vaguely dissatisfied and ... living within quite narrowed boundaries of life," this self views meeting others' expectations as the primary route to maintaining the social standing of a good woman (Schreiber 1996, 475). During the depressive episode, women question the normative assumptions about their femininity and general existence as a subordinated group. In this process of "cluing in," a woman "mak[es] connections" between not only what she knows cognitively, but also what she feels on a "gut level" (Schreiber 1996, 484). Such emotional knowing leads to the realization that parts of herself have been "missing" from her earlier identity. Following this insight, depressed women face a choice—to move toward recovery, which requires a reintegration of those aspects of self that fall outside the narrow confines of being a good, culturally valued woman, or avoiding this process of personal change and social critique by now willfully suppressing what they, on a deeper level, know to be true and in need of attention.

Part of the complexity of depression lies in that it takes the form of dialogues between two voices—a discursively constructed, upbraiding "over-eye," and an empirically grounded self (Crowley Jack 1991). By judging experiential knowledge "in cultural terms" and often invalidating their own viewpoints, women reveal themselves to be immersed in a "vigilant ... self-censoring process" (Crowley Jack 1991, 132, 37), the mechanism through which much of femininity is accomplished (Bartky 1990). However, the presence of dialogues also demonstrates that while entrenched and regularly reinforced, self-policing is also precarious and incomplete. Illustrating such dialogues, one depressed woman evidences the complexity of her subjectivity:

Oh, I'm not a typical Christian woman. I'm a wild hare. I don't do "the good church lady thing" very well. ... Well, not at all, really. ... I know I should, and I tell myself I should try harder, but I just don't seem to do it. (Schreiber 2001, 87)

The dialogue reflects the active attempts of both her voice as a "wild hare" and the discourse of a "typical Christian woman" to establish hegemony over her thoughts and evaluations. While self-recriminating in part, the dialogue is also self-validating. It reveals her existence beyond what she is supposed to be, and prompts her questioning of feminine norms of selflessness and self-sacrifice.

Within the silencing paradigm, full recovery from depression requires uniting a cognitive awareness with subjective knowing, and finding ways to examine whether the external messages women hear are accurate, useful, and inclusive of what they feel and know through experience. Critically sifting through moralistic cultural messages and judgments, women pursuing wellness must determine which they will embrace and which others they will reject as "the not me" (Schreiber 1996). Mental health and wellness therefore hinge upon a woman realizing that the discursive representation of her womanhood fails to incorporate, and thereby distorts, key aspects of her reality as a thinking, acting, and desiring human being. In moving from the disconnection of depression that is also characteristic of much of femininity, women pursuing recovery no longer conceal their realities—their "intelligence, emotions, sexual identities . . . hurts, mistakes, strengths" (Schreiber 2001, 95). Refusing to protect an ideology of femininity, they raise questions about such a standard of goodness whose "*moral authority* [over them] . . . begins to crumble" (Crowley Jack 1991, 196, emphasis in original; see also, LaFrance and Stoppard 2006). As these women come to see that such conventional beliefs are, in fact, lies that have made them sick (Gilligan [1982]1993, xxvi), they can engage their depressions as a healing, temporary, and even "creative [rather than demoralizing] darkness" (Crowley Jack 1991, 192).

Afraid of what they will lose—the regard and praise of others; connection, albeit tenuous and duplicitous, to loved ones; a belief in particular ideologies—women may resort to the emotionally laborious process of "staying clued out" (Schreiber 1996). Such women settle for the familiarity of a "pseudo-recovery," or an ongoing state of disconnection and self-sacrifice to garner their acceptance by others (Schreiber 1996). Continuing to live on two disconnected levels and having thoughts, particularly those prescribed by the ideologies of their social context, that are at odds with their embodied experiences, these women retain an inner/outer split. Doing so, they undertake an intensified suppression of their needs to promote a façade of competence and contentment. Such a strategy upholds cultural ideals of femininity at a cost to their own needs and overall long-term wellness (LaFrance and Stoppard 2006; Mauthner 2002, 13–14).

Depression: The Silences of Black Women's Strength

> Blues about stress and strain could be the Sisters National Anthem. The only time some of us take a break is when we break down.
>
> —Susan Taylor, "Passion for peace"

Although most feminists understand depression as gendered, few have explored how it is also racialized. Thus little work in the silencing paradigm has challenged a prevailing notion of the distress as a *white* woman's illness (see Schreiber, Noerager Stern, and Wilson 1998, 2000 for exceptions). Nor has this developing area of study adequately questioned an implicit corollary to this belief— that Black women, as "strong" women, are culturally protected from depression (Clark Amankwaa 2003a, 2003b; Danquah 1998; Edge and Rogers 2005).

The need for a broader conceptualization of silencing within femininities is evident given the consistent finding in epidemiological studies that racial minority status and poverty are associated with elevated rates of depression among women, particularly during their childbearing and childrearing years (Siefert et al.

2000). Earning less than white women, Black women are also more likely to raise children as single parents and to be poor. Such disparate structural conditions are embedded in Black women's development of clinical depression at rates comparable to white women, and their exhibition of greater levels of subclinical distress than most other race–gender groups (Brown and Keith 2003; Siefert et al. 2000). Further insisting on the need to understand depression as racialized and gendered is the emergence over the last decade of a growing autobiographical and clinical literature focused on the experiences of depressed Black women. Significantly, being strong surfaces as a culturally distinctive aspect of Black women's experiences of the distress (Boyd 1998; Clark Amankwaa 2003b; Danquah 1998; Jones and Shorter-Gooden 2003; Martin 2002; Mitchell and Herring 1998; Schreiber, Noerager Stern, and Wilson 1998, 2000).

In their autobiographical accounts, Black women experiencing depressive episodes[6] draw attention to their strength, which they liken to a performance and a façade rather than a sincere reflection of their experiences. Instead of associating their depression with feelings of helplessness and hopelessness, such women typically emphasize states of extreme psychic and physical exhaustion, frustration, and suppressed anger. Focused on the needs and expectations of others to the neglect of her own, a strong Black woman can become entrapped in a habitual performance of shifting and dissemblance. Long-time *Essence* magazine editor-in-chief Susan Taylor (1995, 7) describes her own depressive episodes as resulting from the extensive accumulation of emotional realities that she felt compelled to withhold:

> With my many fears tenuously contained, I greeted the world each day buffed and polished like the models I presented on the pages of the magazine. My clothing, hair, nails and makeup—all impeccably done, and no one seemed to notice the cracks lengthening beneath the façade of

cheerfulness I wore like armor. I became so skilled at the masquerade that even I began to believe it was real. . . .

I could feel myself withdrawing, wanting to be alone. . . . I could barely look anyone in the eye. I was fighting to keep my cool, my hands steady and my knees strong. I was tired, so tired. Tired of directing, tired of having to answer questions, tired of being Mommy, tired of being the responsible daughter, tired of juggling. Tired of holding in the scream.

When Taylor does release the scream—"my arms flung wide and my head thrown back, it came again and again—a scream that unfurled from the core of my being, carrying my fears, my tears and my frustrations into the wind" (8)—such expression marks the beginning of the healing of her spirit, the start of "loving and nurturing myself" (9). Significantly, self-love and self-care become possible only after dethroning the discourse of strength as a legitimate arbiter of her thinking and feeling. Rejecting the litany of its prescriptions, "that we're born to work, to sacrifice and to serve others, that focusing on our own needs is self-centered and selfish," Taylor (2002a, 5) also refuses to endure strength's embodied effects: "Feeling stressed, anxious and ill [which] have become accepted ways of living for Black women."

Voicing profound concerns for the often hidden, overwrought, and crumbling inner worlds of depressed Black women, Charisse Jones and Kumea Shorter-Gooden (2003) view constant shifting as generating a "Sisterella Complex." Like the mistreated Cinderella, a diligent, self-denying "Sisterella" works "tirelessly, sometimes masochistically, to promote, protect, and appease others." Because she is habituated to self-sacrifice, Sisterella's depression has a "distinctive look."

If you're trying to identify depression in Black women, one of the first things to look for is a woman who is working very hard and seems disconnected from her own needs. She may be busy around the clock, constantly on the go, unable to relax, and often compromising her sleep for household, child-care, and job tasks that she feels impelled to take care of. Not taking the time to tend to herself makes her more vulnerable to depression. Or her busyness may be a way to keep her mind off the feelings of sadness that have already arisen. (125–126)

Sisterella embodies a functional depression. Introjecting the belief that as a strong woman she should concomitantly "dismiss your feelings, distrust your power, [and not] . . . make a fuss" (Taylor 1998, 107), Sisterella engages in the extreme other-directedness and long-term self-neglect characteristic of self-silencing and critical to the emergence of depressive experiences. Black women's continuous overriding of their subjectivity in the name of appearing strong results in the unsettling reality that "[t]he only time some of us take a break is when we break down" (Taylor 2002b, 9).

Black women must struggle against the racialization of depression as a white illness (Boyd 1998; Clark Amankwaa 2003a), even as they are encouraged to racialize struggle as a central manifestation of being authentically Black. Meri Nana-Ama Danquah (1998) shrewdly analyzes this intertwining of the strength and depression discourses that left her, a depressed Black woman, a literal contradiction in terms. She observes that in the racialized gender order, white men's depression is "characterized . . . as a sign of genius," while white women's distress is read through the essentializing lens that they are "idle, spoiled, or just plain hysterical." Following the racist perception of their danger, depressed Black men are "demonized and pathologized" (see also, Head 2004). However, because Black women's intelligibility rides on their emotional and physical resilience or "strength," depression marks them as "weak. And weakness in black women is intolerable" (20). Such weakness violates not only Black women's opposition to white women, but the intraculturally held "claim to superiority . . . [over] 'silly' white people [which is] . . . that [Black people] do not suffer mental illness" (hooks 1993, 70).

Such refusal within and outside of Danquah's community to seeing strong Black women as vulnerable to mental distress permeated discussions of her depression with others. From a white woman, she received the "sarcastic" response: *"Black* women and depression? . . . Isn't that kinda redundant? . . . Don't get me wrong. . . . It's just that when *black* women start going on Prozac, you know the whole world is falling apart" (1998, 19–20). Claiming that Black women are the last defense against human (read white) suffering and therefore the least entitled to fall apart, this response tellingly reflects a social order structured on the backs of mule-like Black women. Such a racist reaction was paralleled by the lack of acknowledgment Danquah received from members of the Black community: "'Girl, you've been hanging out with too many white folk'; 'What do you have to be depressed about? If our people could make it through slavery, we can make it through anything'; 'Take your troubles to Jesus, not no damn psychiatrist'" (21). Thus, the discourses of strength and depression—the first emphasizing Black women's validation through struggle and imperviousness to harm, the second constructing mental distress as largely a white women's prerogative—reinforce each other to deny both the existence and experience of depression among Black women.

Scholar activist bell hooks (1993, 73) recognizes a similar void in the recognition of Black women's suffering. The "breakdown" experienced by a family member at "a moment in her life when she was finding it impossible to cope with parenting" received no sympathy or assistance until, as an addict, she was deemed incapable of caring for her children. hooks insists that this woman was never able to voice, "I am having a nervous breakdown, I can't deal with these children. I need some space to recover myself." Such requests for help and respite "would have gone against the strong black woman norm," and fallen on deaf, unresponsive ears.

However, in the culturally recognized sick role of addict, this woman "was perceived as being 'out of control,' no longer a 'good' parent and it was acceptable for her to abandon her children to the care of other family members." Rather that frame this as an isolated case of distress, hooks (1993, 73) maintains that addictions generally may be a strategy "to take needed time out," utilized by those women—particularly among the poor and working class—viewed as too strong to need assistance from others. Because depression is not an acceptable illness among African Americans and particularly not among Black women, emotional distress may be forced into more culturally acceptable behavioral forms (Head 2004; Jones and Shorter-Gooden 2003).

What emerges from these autobiographical accounts of depression is that Black women feel themselves intensely silenced and submerged under prescriptions of strength. At times it is friends and family who censure Black women with the familiar characterization of depression as a white woman's illness and thus, if experienced, a sign of a Black woman's inauthenticity. However, equally problematic are Black women's internalized practices of surveillance that accord putting others at ease with goodness, and self-concern with selfishness and whiteness. Taken in by these lies of strength, these Black women believe that their "wounds [are] just another proof of [their] strength and invulnerability" (Wallace [1978]1990, 108). Such claims rest on the assumption that Black women are more body than mind and not fully human. In this encouragement of selflessness, strength—like other discourses of femininity—places Black women at risk for ongoing self-silencing, self-policing, and eventual depression.

Conclusion

A critical finding over the last twenty years of feminist work is that women's bodies hold multivalent meaning. They are obvious objects of domination and discipline under the racialized regimes of femininity. However, by listening carefully against the grain of femininities, a number of feminist scholars have emphasized the continuum between normative and distressed womanhood, and the ways in which the body can express both overwhelming cultural pressures and piercing social critiques.

Women's common experiences of embodied distress—such as eating problems and depression—evidence both subordination and resistance. Read as pathologies, they emphasize the disciplinary force of femininities to drive women to extremes of distraction and disorder. However, as a growing feminist literature maintains, such problems of the mind and body can also be read as acts of self-protection, and reflect women's attempts to subvert the feminine constraints imposed on them. Eating patterns that reduce or enlarge the body's size can protest violence and compromised opportunities and, in the process, attempt to make room for women to exist outside of the narrow confines of a femininity. Similarly, as a breakdown in a woman's ability to carry on feminine responsibilities, depression can also manifest women's unconscious scrutiny of and challenges to those expectations. Thus the physical body and mind can be brought to bear on both the doing and the undoing of racialized gender (Deutsch 2007; West and Zimmerman 1987), in experiences of health as well as sickness.

For Black women, both eating problems and depression take hold while they are dutifully performing their femininity, being the capable, loving, and resilient persons others expect them to be. The genesis of these problems involves the recognition on an internal level that the women cannot live up to the image of strength and that significant aspects of their experiences are allowed no voice or validation through their acts of invulnerability. While denied expression through the normative performance of strength, these feelings of frustration, fear, overwork, anger, and despair do exist. Without the support and the language to express the turmoil within, strong Black women's discrepant feelings become embodied as distresses, but rarely gain the status of such given the racialized framing of eating problems and depression as white women's illnesses. Furthermore, these distresses are too often denied by the women themselves and thus rendered into another burden to carry, yet another act in one's performance of strength.

Because Black women are allowed very restricted terms for their recognition as "good" women, claims of their strength are tied much more forcefully to their domination rather than to their subversion of or liberation from the dualisms of race and gender. However, by bringing the suffering of Black women to light, the autobiographical accounts of compulsive overeating and depression challenge tenets of the racialized gender order. Speaking about their complete subjectivity, Black women admitting their vulnerability resist their formulation as other-than-human and exceptional in ways that preclude their exploitation and suffering. They contest the racialized Cartesian split that consistently accords subordinated groups a lesser humanity in relation to their privileged counterparts, and reveal "strength" to be a cruel and indefensible ruse.

Denied their own validity and existence, Black women's bodies are routinely used as repositories for society's most challenging and least recognized emotion work. Such bodies are respected for their ability to care for others who can lay a moral claim to their efforts. Overeating, continued self-silencing, subsequent overweight, and active yet denied depression, then, can be usefully understood as tools of the ideological "machinery" (Bartky 1990) that converts and contorts a Black woman's body into a strong one. Consequently, the weight-related diseases that plague the Black female community (e.g., adult-onset diabetes, heart disease, and hypertension) may not be symptoms of the "lifestyle" problems of overeating, lack of exercise, or unhealthy diet. Instead, they may reflect a consistent level of abuse in social relations that treat Black women, in their communities as well as in the larger society, as literal beasts of burden. In order to explore how strength comes to dictate such limited terms of existence for Black women, I now turn to a voice-centered analysis of the interview data.

3 / Keeping Up Appearances

The Performance of Strength

And I think that *strong woman* idea has been
planted in my head, too. That you're supposed to be
able to, you know, just muster through this, and,
you know, make it without scarring or whatever.

> —Jennifer, twenty-nine, divorced mother,
>   bank employee

My mom. She, she real strong. . . . And, my mom
will work, and I think her only downfall was that
she worked and she helped to take care of everybody else's kids, too. . . . She just, she *always* tried to
help other people. And I think, sometimes, Black
women get *used* by trying to help other people. . . .
You know, it's like, Black women just think they're
everybody's mother.

> —Angie, twenty-four, single, student

We think that if we're not this superwoman, we
kind of, we'll put the blame on *ourselves*, for not
being able to accomplish all these things. And try
to be this twenty-four-hour woman, that everybody,
you know, society kind of makes you believe you
have to be. . . . Whether it would be your partner, or
your mother putting the, "You know, *I* did it, so
why can't you do it?" you know.

> —Kiki, twenty-four, single mother,
>   medical technician

S trength is a prescriptive discourse. As the preceding quotes collectively underscore, a strong Black woman should "muster through" all adversity "without scarring," should "*always* [try] to help other people," and should present herself as a capable "twenty-four-hour woman" regardless of the demands and stresses she faces. Particularly noteworthy is the open-endedness of this mandate for silent, ongoing struggle. There is very little, if any, sense of limits as to what can be expected of a "strong Black woman."

Strength introjects unremitting adversity—whether due to financial strains, workplace injustices, or relational abuses—into validating tests of Black women's authenticity among family and peers. Marie, a divorced, thirty-nine-year-old educator who has taken in others' children, remarks that when people claim that a Black woman is strong, "nobody seems to understand that you are *striving* to stay afloat.... And I can even see it, in relationship to Black men.... The person doesn't see that, you know, *you* need some assistance with your load. The person's like, 'You don't need anything. *I* need you to take care of me.'" Rendering Black women's subjective points of view immaterial, strength encourages them to "put the blame on ourselves" for not measuring up to the standards and circumstances seen as synonymous with Black womanhood.

"Being strong" obliges Black women to exhibit a ready endurance to a life constructed against the backdrop of obstacles, unfairness, and, tellingly, a lack of assistance from others. Drawing on the historical reality of slavery and the continuing economic and political marginalization of African Americans, this imperative has much merit: It foregrounds daily and real struggles for security, health, wellness, and choice, which too easily are forgotten or minimized in mainstream discourses of a post-civil rights, colorblind, and finally democratic United States (Hill Collins 2005). For many Black women, then, exhibiting strength is not consciously encountered as a problematic or an arbitrary framing of their lives. Facing adversity amidst extensive caretaking responsibilities are common realities evident in the actions of the kin and friends whom Black women love and respect, and after whom they model themselves. As a result, to become a strong Black woman is to follow a well-worn and distinguished path of hard work, caring, faithfulness, and generosity—the most tangible and revered example of Black womanhood.

As a racialized construction of gender, claims of strength by and about Black women not only emphasize their authenticity but their superiority over other women and men based on their abilities to weather all manner of hardship. However, the ideological interests of the discourse are revealed in the ways it polices Black women's experiences to accord with the racialized boundaries of gender it upholds. The normalization of struggle plays a critical role in marking a Black woman's strength so that women without observable or adequate adversity in their lives become contradictory figures. Their characterization by family and peers as "weak," not Black, or "white" expresses moral admonishment for behavior or circumstances deemed inconsistent with authentic Black womanhood (Henson Scales 2001). And within the logic of the unforgiving dualisms that work against acknowledging human variability and fault in social structures, such "anomalies" need to be "re-racilialise[d]" or recategorized as non-Black or white (Du Cille 2001, 417). Racializing womanhood in such ways, the discourse of strength intensively labors to "maintain the illusion of strict racial borders and not betray the constructed nature of race in general" (Shaw 2005, 148). In the process, neither the associations of authentic Black womanhood with financial struggle (and white women with material security) are contested, nor is space within this dichotomous framework allowed to understand and appreciate *any* woman's actual experiences.[1]

Illuminating the racialized boundaries of strength, Jennifer discusses how her cousin, a successful business owner, is perceived by family as "livin' the white life" and is consequently called "white girl":

> She drives a nice car; she's got her money. I don't know what *emotional* struggles she has, but in appearance, she's always, you know, well-to-do. And that's a "white girl," you know, because she's not [struggling].

Specific aspects of the cousin's life—her financial security, international travel, lack of children, or faithful husband—could each be singled out for rendering her status as a real Black woman questionable. Such are at odds with what the discourse mandates: Explains Jennifer, "[B]eing a Black woman means, you know, you're at home, you struggle, you get out *once in a while*, and that's supposed to be *meaningful* to you. You're not *supposed* to, you know, go and do, or whatever." The discourse insists that struggle is a predetermined fixture in Black women's lives. As a result, it entrenches class boundaries between racialized genders and individualizes ongoing social inequities into litmus tests of race membership. Within the discourse, the challenges many Black women face are not scrutinized as indictments of the society or of particular social relationships. Instead, race conflated with class is accorded the valence of a natural rather than socially constructed phenomenon.

Reflecting on who and what earns the distinction of strength among Black women, Joy, a thirty-two-year-old college administrator, identifies similar intimate connections between a culturally valued Black womanhood and life-defining hardship:

> We're always *doing* it alone, and the men can't come through, and *now* I'm strong. But how many women whose husbands come through are strong? . . . I'm saying the definition of strength *within* the Black paradigm includes lack of self-care *and* lack of a partner. It's difficult to assert

yourself—as a *married Black woman* in a stable relationship—as a strong woman, unless you have an *abundance*
of kids or something where you work two or three jobs.

Such a critique of the struggles viewed as essential to "being
strong" is not a denial of the material constraints in many Black
women's lives. In fact, like the overwhelming majority of the women
interviewed and a significant proportion of Black women in society, Joy and Jennifer had been raised in working-class families
toiling in underpaid, economically vulnerable jobs. Their own experiences of social mobility into the lower echelons of the middle
class were typically recent and more evident in their perseverance
and optimism than in their attainment of material security. In
other words, they were not removed from the economic ravages of
racism.

What concerns these women is the extent to which Black communities and the larger society embrace economic inequality and
extensive, solitary struggle as a distinguishing feature of Black
womanhood. Strength exalts Black women's tireless support for
others and presumed inability to experience resentment, fear, or
anger. Such expectations of essential difference create a fertile
ground for inequality (Risman 2004). That is, when silently bearing up to demands is deemed the appropriate response to *all* circumstances, Black women are easily placed in situations that no
one should have to endure.

The moral parameters set up by strength prescribe that no
"good" woman would focus on herself when struggle is omnipres-
ent, the needs of others so profound, and the capacities of such a
"strong" woman so limitless. Within this construction, undertak-
ings that generate self-knowledge, support joy and creativity, or
encourage critiques of strength are dismissed as "superfluous . . .
frou-frou" and devoid of "any value." The logic of the strength discourse in what Joy calls "the Black paradigm" insists that "It's *fine*
to have a dream as a Black woman as long as it's being deferred.

You can have all the dreams you want—'Girl, when I get on my feet, I just can't wait until I can get me some rest.' You can have all these dreams, but it can't be actualizing, or you've neglected someone else." Equating strength so closely with ever-present struggles and the needs of others tells a woman that there are always greater, more meaningful concerns than what she is feeling inside and what she can imagine or want for herself. Such a combination of hardship, caretaking, and selflessness leaves Black women vulnerable to becoming, as thirty-six-year-old Aisha describes, "make-do women," who manage unjust circumstances with a quiet dignity.

Picking Up My Mother's Strength

> We were taught that you really didn't show your feelings that much. You kind of kept things inside and dealt with them. . . . [The] main thing was taught that, whatever it is, overcome it, deal with it, and go ahead on.
>
> —Traci, forty-three, divorced mother

Black women are largely introduced to the discourse of strength through the example and directives of mothers. Such women are typically held in high regard for managing multiple life challenges with grace and wells of love for others in their care. As discussed in the following quote, Traci's term "picking up . . . strength" reflects a process through which she and other women come to see themselves as capable of moving into their mothers' examples of womanhood.

> From childhood. Even from, just say a young girl. You go to school. You know, you don't want to go to school in kindergarten because it's just, "Oh, I'm scared." "You're not scared." They drop you off, you look back at mom, and you're sad. "Okay, I'm going into this new world. I have to deal with it." . . . It's just something you just *learn*. You try

to instill in yourself. "Well, mom told me to be strong, so I have to be strong like her." And then you start following the example. And then once you see mom strong, grandmother strong, you very seldom see them cry that much. *I* very seldom saw them cry that much, but the *strength* was there. And that's just, you just pick it up. And the next thing you know, what mom is doing, you're trying to do it. And just about everything. You see her cooking, you try to cook. You see her cleaning, you try to clean [chuckle].

Speaking of her own childhood in the second person, Traci highlights strength as a general cultural prescription that girls encounter—"It's just something you just *learn*." By observing and carefully mimicking a mother's actions, a girl hopes to eventually master a similar self-assurance and override her internal fears. Shows of strength, as defined by a sense of calm and self-control, preclude the expression of deep emotion. "To be strong like" your mother means "following the example" of women whom "you very seldom see . . . cry that much." In picking up strength, concerns and needs at odds with the discourse are dismissed as private matters that should have no bearing on what one does as a "strong Black woman." Significantly, in accommodating to strength, Traci literally takes on her mother's voice—"'You're not scared'"—as a guide for her own thought and behavior. However, such ventriloquation (Brown 1998) does not eradicate her initial and ongoing worries. Instead, like other women, she learns to speak and act on the words of strength while denying her real feelings.

Picking up strength is a process of accommodation. Black women learn to gauge themselves by external standards and monitor their outward behavior in the presence of others. Over time, such women become skilled in relegating fears, anger, and personal needs to an interior space, what Crystal in the Introduction describes as her "deep down inside." The splits between what a woman does and how she feels, between others' perceptions and her own become a way of managing a racialized and gendered social order in which her desires and interests, as a multiply marginalized person, are deemed to have no social consequence. Such accommodations and the subsequent separation of actions from feelings are ongoing. While this process of dissociation begins under a mother's tutelage, it quickly becomes a well-practiced "habit of survival" (Scott 1991), employed at home, in heterosexual relationships, and in majority-white workplaces. As a result, women accommodating to strength speak of being actresses, wearing masks, living behind walls, and burying deeply felt but strength-discrepant emotions within themselves.

Dichotomous thinking buttresses the concept of strength as the antithesis of being weak, whiny, or acting like a white woman. Describes Rita, a thirty-five-year-old graduate student:

> [Being strong is] almost *ingrained* in you from day [one]. You know, you don't cry easily. If something happens, you get up. You don't cry. You don't let it bother you. "Get over it." You know, I don't know how many times I've heard that. "Oh, you'll be alright." And, in fact, you know, that's also why when we think of white women, stereotypically . . . we think of them as being weak because they cry all the time. And in fact, I also find myself, "Why are you crying? Get over it. Let it go." . . . If I see someone, a white woman crying or something like that, you know, I'll catch myself because [chuckle] she has a right to cry. Or feel the way she feels. And I think that part of being a strong Black woman is . . . that you become desensitized to your own feelings about things.

What Rita refers to as the "*ingrain*[ing]" of strength takes the form of learning to talk to oneself through an insistent, unyielding language spoken particularly forcefully by mothers and girlfriends.

Among the people closest to her, Rita has learned not to have or expect authentic relationships—those that allow her to express a range of feelings and needs, to speak in a language of "strengths" and "weaknesses." Rita's criticism of phrases of encouragement— "'Get over it.... Oh, you'll be alright.'"—is that they are typically deployed to draw attention away from hurt and refocus Black girls and women on tasks and responsibilities at hand. Such responses force back underground those very same feelings that the unfair expectations of strength create. Consequently, Black women learn to "become desensitized to your own feelings about things." Held to more flexible standards, a white woman has the right to cry, a recognized prerogative to "feel the way she feels." Her inner world matters and when revealed to others can garner sympathetic responses. However, given the evaluation of crying as a sign of weakness that invalidates one's claim to Black womanhood, the discourse of strength effectively leaves no space in which a woman, like Rita, can admit woundedness. Habituated to the silencing uses of strength, Rita concludes that for a Black woman, "strength is really *defined by what you do*," rather than how she feels or what she wants.

Raised by a mother who is "not a person that can talk about weakness" and is "not one to show emotions," thirty-nine-year-old Guerline struggles "to really *show* when I'm hurting, depressed." Years of following her mother's example and picking up strength impede her expression of feelings contrary to her strength persona:

> I don't intune into my own emotional state. I always try to, I've always, I've always kept things in. And it just builds and builds and builds. Either I would become very. Uhhhh, I would become, I would be *angry*, and my anger would go toward people I care [about]. This is a problem that *I* have to learn. If I'm hurting, and I should just say, "I'm hurting." If I'm *crying*, I should allow the tears to come out.

The idea of revealing her fears and disappointments rubs up against Guerline's socialization, which has left her feeling "that I always had to be together. I had to be. I always had to be *strong*, and that's the way I felt. That's the way I *feel*." For Guerline, being strong is an extreme state. It requires a woman to be composed at all times, under all circumstances. A moment of crying or anger, in Guerline's thinking and in that of many others, calls into question one's image as a good woman, a strong woman, and "take[s] away from who you are." However, the active struggle of Guerline's inner world against the mandate of strength reflects a beginning realization that what is good for her can include feeling what she feels, rather than only the imperative to always show strength. As she states, being able to recognize her anger and hurt in relationships is a "problem that *I* have to learn."

Direct instruction in shows of fortitude precludes Black women's comfort with employing other self-presentations, particularly if mothers took a tough line with them. Performing strength requires silences and dissociations within and between Black women. Because strong mothers establish the example of invulnerability by so carefully guarding the range of emotions they experience, a resulting disconnect emerges between a daughter's respect for her mother and the intimacy she feels with her role model (Joseph 1981; Ward 1996). Without evidence of their mothers' humanity, Black daughters are thereby left to question their own. Maturing into adulthood, they come to see their doubts, hurts, and worries as problematic weaknesses incongruent with these closely observed and highly revered models of Black female goodness.

Demonstrating little outward compassion for their daughters' mistakes and encouraging them to learn hard life lessons, these mothers emphasize that good women are responsible and that particularly, as *Black* women in a racist society, it is both foolish and disempowering for girls to expect that others will provide assistance, rescue, or even compassionate understanding. Remembering a time when she and other family members accidentally consumed contaminated seafood, Jennifer reveals how her mother handled the situation to insist on a larger point—her accountability for all outcomes from her actions.

> I was about five years old. . . . Well, when I was little, we got real sick, 'cause I remember going to get the needles in my side, because that's how they tested your blood for your liver. And this all came behind some oysters. But anyway, I was a greedy kid, and my *mom* . . . was over cooking for us. And she had made some okra. At the other side, we had chicken soup, and I didn't want no chicken soup. 'Cause I want to eat some *okra*, right? They have shrimps in there! Lobsters, you know! . . . My mother said, "Don't eat that." And I said, "I'm hungry. There ain't no more soup." I ate and I ended up bringing it back up. *Do you know my mom made me clean that up!* She had *no sympathy* for me whatsoever! [chuckle].

In her narrative, Jennifer underscores her own childhood indignation—*"Do you know my mom made me clean that up!"*— and deems as callous her mother's response of *"no sympathy."* She also portrays her mother's actions as extreme and inappropriate for the situation, given her young age and the fact that her uncle almost died from exposure to the hepatitis virus in the seafood. From this incident, the message that Jennifer learned from her mother's actions and which she has carried forward into her adulthood is that a Black girl is responsible for all that befalls her regardless of the actual causes of the troubles.

Significantly, although Jennifer expresses disbelief and a palpable outrage about her mother's framing and handling of the situation, she also demonstrates a resignation to this childrearing practice. At the end of her account, she tellingly draws parallels between this experience as a child and an episode from her own parenting.

> And I have *dragged* that right through my life to my daughter's. I mean, she was there, had puked her little guts out, and I'm like, "Girl, get me the dustpan! You should have used the trash can." I'm trippin'.

Jennifer knows strength expectations are fraudulent in their use of painful situations to convince Black daughters to be vigilant about their decisions and actions. Furthermore, she evaluates her own use of such childrearing practices as an instance of "trippin'" or of being unreasonable. However, she also concludes that such practices are "built in. If we ever change it, I won't be here to see it." In spite of her awareness of the unfairness of such treatment of young Black girls, her behavior as a mother remains largely culturally prescribed, so powerful are the norms that insist on raising girls to be strong.

Women reflecting on their upbringings disclose that the strength they were groomed to demonstrate often took the form of being "raised . . . like *men*." This statement reveals that Black girls and women, who are expected to be the backbone of families and communities, are taught to combine the caretaking responsibilities of women ("because, of course, we were going to be raising the kids") with the emotional fortitude and self-reliance associated with men. With regard to her own stepdaughter, Tasha, a thirty-three-year-old married police officer, describes the logic of this strategic upbringing:

> I make her hang with the boys. I do. Because I don't want her to be a sissy. . . . Yeah, I mean, I don't want her to be, you know, whiny. I want her to be out there, you know, to go and be able to take care of herself. . . . If she gets into anything or whatever, I want her to be able to handle it.

Other women share Tasha's interest in raising daughters to be "tomboys," rather than "sissies," so that they learn to project not simply competence and responsibility, but an emotional invulnerability from a young age. This seemingly androgynous upbringing appears liberating, as these girls engage in self-supporting activities conventionally associated with boys and avoid the excessive and often crippling dependence of hegemonic white femininity. However, within families and communities, such childrearing is easily exploited. Strong girls and women are often encouraged to think of themselves primarily as the emotional and financial caretakers of the men in their lives, and to associate self-care and concern with weakness and selfishness.

Fostering a view of self as impervious to adversity can inadvertently habituate Black girls and young women to a life filled with double standards and a lack of concern for them as human beings who can be hurt and who should not be harmed. Jennifer recalls that when "your parents tell you, 'Shut up. You better not cry,'" such a response largely parallels the views of the larger society that has long imagined Black women as devoid of the emotional capacities and therefore the vulnerabilities and overall humanity of white women and men. Despite the good intentions of Black families to protect their daughters by steeling them against a naive reliance on others, the construction of strength as a combination of masculine capability and feminine responsibility has its own blind spots. Because the role of "being strong" rests on external rather than self-identified definitions of being all things to all people, it renders Black women's relationships to others into flexible, ever-expanding circles of obligation. Recognized for what they do, not how they feel, strong Black women are confined by a discourse that speaks in extremes—always giving, never complaining; ever strong, never weak. Having to "pick up" strength and hide discrepant emotions from view initiates Black girls into a world in which much of their actual experience consistently fails to become part of the official "story" of their lives (Gilligan 2006, 57).

Men and Children First

Developing strength among daughters leads mothers to encourage them to be the emotional, physical, and often financial caretakers of kin. This is a particularly gendered message that women describe as leaving men virtually free from having to honor commitments to the women in their lives. Critiquing how her mother's example "trained [me] to . . . put everything I need to get *for me* on the back burner," Angie explains how extensive caretaking becomes women's work:

> Angie: They always say, "You gotta be there for your family." And that's the worst thing. I tell my momma that. "That's the worst thing you could teach a person."
> TB: Why? And when you say "a person," is it that they teach the sons and the daughters that? Or is it that a daughter [hears this as telling her] . . .
> Angie: They teach, they teach their children that. And it's how we interpret it. They teach the son that, "You gotta be there for each other," and I think sons listen to it as, "You can screw up, they [the women] got your back." Whereas daughters listen to it as, "I got to *take care* of. I got to watch out for my brother. I got to watch out for my family."

Angie remarks that the notion of feeling responsible for family reassures boys and men that the girls and women in their families will provide them with a safety net of unconditional support to cushion them from the consequences of their behavior. For their part, girls hear the message as instructing them to be vigilantly attentive to the needs of others. Such a message leaves little room for a girl to comfortably "screw up" like her brothers, or to identify needs of her own. In preparing them to be caring sisters, mothers, partners, or wives, strength reinforces the sexist belief that "we're

protectors, we're *supposed* to be there. We're supposed to put ourselves last, and all the other stuff." As such, by mandating social
motherhood and a compulsory heterosexuality (Rich 1980), these
care demands are a visceral reminder that strong Black women are
still women, subject to a male-defined view of family life and
gender-appropriate behaviors.

The patriarchal investment in strength as selfless caretaking is
poignantly illuminated in Crystal's account of how her father and
brothers placed the burden of tending to her dying mother squarely
and solely on her "strong" shoulders:

> They wouldn't do anything. And I was taking my kids late
> [to school], I was not doing well in school, I was just, chaos.
> And, I looked at my dad. I couldn't keep my eyes open. He
> say, "*You* don't need any *help*! My son[s], I mean, your
> *brothers*, they have to *work*; you're not going to pay their
> bills." And then, I was like, "I just want some sleep." [Ad-
> dressing her mother, he said,] "She don't want you here!"
> just because I say I need some sleep. . . . He said I didn't
> need any rest or sleep. And my *brothers* didn't have to do
> anything.

Called a "superwoman," Crystal was consequently deemed not to
have any recognized need for relief. Her simple desire for "some
sleep" was distorted by her father into a reproachful rejection of
her mother. By presuming strength of Crystal, the men in her family avoided the emotional and physical labor of tending to her
mother, a highly regarded strong Black woman. Because Crystal's
needs were automatically interpreted as signs of selfishness, her only
recourse to maintain her standing as a dutiful daughter and strong
Black woman was to neglect her exhaustion and silently accept a
wholly inequitable caretaking load. She later remarks that it is
largely male kin and romantic partners who attribute such strength
to her and in the process completely invalidate her needs for as-

sistance. This pattern reflects in large part that it is men who stand to gain from a social organization that defines significant and ongoing caretaking as the specific labors of "strong" women.

Having undergone a similar experience of nursing both of her dying parents, largely without the emotional or material assistance of her brothers, Rita now views charges of weakness as a tactic to keep a strong woman in her place of subordinating her needs to those of others, particularly men.[2]

> Weakness is really someone who doesn't contribute to *men* the way, you know, *men* expect it to happen. And I see that especially in the church. You know, if you don't support men in the church, then, you know, what kind of woman are you? . . . Or if you don't have a man or support . . . something that a man is doing in the community, then what kind of person are you?

Women who run the risk of incurring indictments for their non-strong or selfish behavior are those who do not adequately concern themselves with male desires, are not demonstrably heterosexual, or are simply cognizant of their own needs outside the care of others. Upheld by such proscriptions are patriarchal family dynamics in which loved ones in a woman's network *"don't see you as human. It's like you're a continually functioning machine,"* remarks Aisha. From observing such exploitation of her mother, Aisha concludes that "[to be a strong Black woman] you have to die to yourself. And let everybody else live. And help them live. That's what our community tells us."

> TB: So, the way you die to yourself [is]? How would I know a woman has "died to herself"?
>
> Aisha: When you see her working two and three jobs, taking crap that, you know, nobody in their right mind should be taking, but she takes it with a smile on her

face and keeps going, and is just, you know, just handling everything, you know, without. She complains
about it, but at the same time, she's doing it.

Aisha's phrase of "dying to herself" vividly depicts the internal
deterioration that occurs while a Black woman ministers to all
placed in her care. Such self-sacrifice reflects the steady erosion
of an experience-based standpoint from which a woman could
evaluate, question, and potentially oppose the demands being put
upon her. Despite being extensive, the wear of strength—which
dictates terms of ongoing self-sacrifice to Black women—is largely
invisible to others. Because a strong woman is taught to focus on
her outward behavior and not reveal discrepant emotions, she
undertakes—even in her distress—the endless workloads of "just
handling everything" for others "with a smile." Placing determina-
tions of her goodness in the hands of others, rather than rooting
them in her own standards of value, she is left with little choice
but to concede to expectations that she should "tak[e] crap that you
know nobody in their right mind should be taking." Saddled with
excessive demands and allowed no recognized way to challenge
the inequality in her relationships, such a woman is rendered into
little more than a mule at work for others.

In two-parent families, the strength-induced selflessness of
working Black mothers can direct them to cover over relational
and financial realities that would suggest that their homes are not
in patriarchal order. Such women may place their earnings in the
family fund and publicly—in front of children and friends—ask
husbands for money to purchase household necessities or personal items and services. Others may quietly and unassumingly
supplement the shortfalls in their husband's income to maintain
not only financial security, but the men's image as breadwinner.

Referring to her home country of Haiti, sixty-two-year-old So-
phie reveals that it was not uncommon for married women to accept that it was beneath their husband to "go or do [just] anything"

to support their family. As a result, a dutiful and strong woman would typically engage in whatever work she could find, and might even have affairs with other men to bring in income "so she could take care of her husband. . . . To clothe . . . and feed him and things like that. . . . And she didn't see anything bad about it." Strong women also include those who endure marital infidelity and abuse for the sake of sustaining the illusion of a functional family unit. Through these efforts of minimizing attention to their own activities and concessions, Aisha finds that Black women enable children to "think your father is on a *pedestal*. . . . But you don't really see the underlying sacrifices your mother *made* to keep him on that pedestal." In these contexts of patriarchal family rule, strength is a strategy, an effective way of keeping afloat families defined by male privilege and female service, an ideology that sees "menial" work as acceptable for a good Black woman but insulting to the masculinity of a good Black man.

The endurance of strong Black women is rarely focused on their own achievement or their own well-being. They are strong *for* others, but often struggle to act with a similar conviction to name and pursue their own needs. From a decade of managing the long-term illnesses of loved ones, forty-five-year-old Morgan explains how she feels like "an over-milked cow. An over-fished river." Physically and emotionally reeling from the recent diagnosis of an aggressive cancer, she bristles at the persistent use of strength to say "we don't need anything. Not even basic understanding and compassion":

I'm tired. . . . So it's like I'm so *damned tired*. . . . But we don't get that time and it's like, if we don't *take* it, as women of color, we don't get it. No one allows us to rest. . . . And it's, it's like they want to penalize you for just being human. And I know in my own church, when I found out that I had the lumps in my breast . . . *no one* comes to me and says, "How are you?" In fact, some people are actually

> insulted because I haven't accepted this or that responsibil-
> ity to the church. They're like, "Oh well, you should just be
> superwoman and rise above it."

Appeals to her strength deny her need for care, her exhaustion from caring for others, and her right to determine for whom she will care. Noteworthy in her example is that the fortifying aspects of religion are invoked not to encourage Morgan in her pursuit of the healing of her body, but rather to justify endless demands of *"dumping* on you, *dumping* on you, poisoning you. From *every angle.* And the thing is, when you say, 'I don't want to be poisoned anymore,' or you don't *hide* it that you're overwhelmed, then they find you abhorrent and weak and [say], 'Oh, how dare you be weak? How dare you need help? How dare you say, 'I can't do this?'"

Morgan's experiences highlight a common gendered logic within Christian Black communities—"no cross, no crown"— which extols self-sacrifice as a "natural, virtuous, even glorious" standard of redemption reserved solely for the women (Weems 2004, 162). What is problematic about such expectations is that they reinforce the selflessness that pervades these women's lives outside of church. As Jennifer observes, majority female church congregations *"fixed* on whatever this *preacher* is telling them they should do" hear a message that supports the continued negation of their needs. Subsequently, it is "very *easy"* for them to conclude, "'Why worry about me? You know, my job on this earth is to take care of everybody else. And God's going to fix it for me.'"

Acknowledging the male-centeredness of families and community institutions built upon their self-sacrifice is often difficult for Black women. Given their socialization to emphasize racial solidarity, they can view gender as a divisive, secondary, and often racially irrelevant concern (Hill Collins 2005; Sizemore 1973). However, Jennifer's discussion of Black women turning to lesbian relationships places in relief and indirectly challenges the accommodations that many women feel are necessary in heterosexual unions.

> There was a woman who did an article that I was reading in this book, about why she became a lesbian. The different factors and reasons, and she says it wasn't all about *women* being like *beaten*, you know, so much as opposed to women being fed up. . . . We are *socialized* to expect a Black woman to be able to take the things she takes. So, [a Black man] has like a *blindfold* on when she's really going through all these things. Whereas *she* felt with being with another woman, they both have suffered the same things. They both have been, you know, having to be these super-women, and she said now she can relax. You know, it's *okay* if she breaks down and *cries* in the middle of the night, because, you know, she don't know where her bill money is coming from or whatever. Or, it's *okay* if she wakes up and says she doesn't want to dress her kids or doesn't want to iron their clothes, because she's just so tired, she just don't really give a la-la. Because *now* this other woman understands how she feels. . . . Now, it was a real interesting article.

Jennifer emphasizes the existence of a reciprocity that few of the interviewees experienced with male partners or even with female friends who subscribed to strength as a valid expectation of Black women. Cognizant of how she cannot reveal herself or her vulnerable emotions to others, Jennifer is drawn to the potential of lesbian relationships to recognize a woman's feelings and to allow her to "relax," "brea[k] down," and "*cr[y]* in the middle of the night" in front of a loved one. The possibility of mutuality in an intimate relationship is not only "interesting" but disruptive of heterosexist norms. It is therefore a threat to the conditions of strength that obscure Black women's realities from men and minimize them to themselves. The actions of her friends who have left marriages and found lesbian relationships, as well as the testimonies in the book, corroborate many of the desires that Jennifer and others express: to be in relationships embedded in a "progressive gender ideology" (Hill Collins 2005) that will not leave them exhausted and feeling disparaged among loved ones.

Mammy Me?: Strong Black Women at Work

Oppositional and racialized constructions of gender are quite obvious to Black women, particularly when employed as one of a few, often token, women of color in majority-white organizations. They eloquently describe the ways in which the jobs they perform are rewritten to include the care and security of coworkers and employers. The mammification to which Black women are most subject is particularly evident in contrast to the treatment of white women in these workplaces. Claims of Black women's strength force the contrast between Black laborers/mules and white ladies of leisure, in what Aida Hurtado (1989) terms the "dual construction of womanhood." As a result, Black women often find that at work, their social role is, as forty-seven-year-old Marva describes, "to be the comfort person. And to be the one who, 'Oh, it's a burning fire in there. And there's a kid. Here, you go get it,' you know."

The only African American employee at a factory, Marva notes that she is continually singled out as a "woman" while white coworkers are accorded a relatively privileged "ladylike" status. Claims of her strength perpetuate a false and inequitable distinction between the predominantly working-class employees.

And working here and working other places, they always think of you being a strong Black woman, so we can come bring *anything* to your door. Because you can handle that.

But we won't give the *same thing* to the lady standing next to you. . . . [Although] we're [the female employees] coming in at the *same size* [physically], doing the *same job*. . . . But because *she whines*, we're not going to put it on her, because it might break her. Because she can't *stand* all that. . . . But, you know, let's give it to her. She can handle it. She's a strong Black woman. Here you go.

Attributing strength to Marva is a rhetorical strategy that secures her exploitation by employers and coworkers. It is, as Marva observes, a "backhand compliment" that initially "tickles your ears. So you're thinking, 'Ooh, that's good. I want to be a strong Black woman.' So you let them dump, and dump, and dump, and then finally you think, 'No, I'm not. If that's what I get for being that, then I'm not.' " Extolling the strength of Black women is a ploy used, as Sheila similarly observes in her majority-white university setting, "to put more on you. To *assume* that you want to do this, and not *say* anything."

Although Marva does not protest her mistreatment by complaining—a tactic regularly and successfully utilized by the white "ladies"—she also suspects that there are no acceptable means for objection given that she is a Black woman. "If I whined and threw a big fit, I probably wouldn't have a *job*. Because I *'refused* to run something'. . . . I've *never* whined. I do it here [at home], but I don't do it there, because it doesn't change anything." As Marva explains, complaining among Black women runs the risk of being dismissed as insubordination, often by enlisting the assistance of another controlling image, the Angry Black Woman, to deny specific relational violations.

It's like [either I'm the] the *angry* Black woman, or I'm the *strong* Black woman. And you're [white co-workers] more happy with the strong one, 'cause you know what you can do to her. She'll take it all. But the *angry* Black woman . . .

[says], "Today, I don't care. Today I'm not trying to pacify
you, and I'm not trying to get by".... And you can't be
anybody else.... [But] *none* of those people are me. I am
just *me*.

The choice handed to many Black women is a false and empty
one: To remain strong is to silently accept unfair workplace dynamics; to speak up about such practices is to be chastised as "angry" and summarily dismissed.[3] Both options enable people to
"put you in a box" observes Nita, a thirty-six-year-old higher education administrator. The easy use of these controlling images as the
only terms of Black women's participation in workplaces essentially means for Celia, a forty-year-old health educator, that "you
aren't standing up for yourself." As a result, she experiences constant internal fears that "you've agreed to too much. You've lis-
tened to one too many insults without, you know, *bringing* the
balance back to say, 'Whoa. Stop it. This is my limit.'" For such
women, their acceptance as a coworker and success as an employee is predicated on contributing to their own exploitation.

Understanding that mammies are considered "help" and never
taken seriously as peers or supervisors nor viewed as legitimate
sources of knowledge, Black women often feel that the only way to
contest this image is to "armor" (Edmondson Bell and Nkomo 1998)
themselves in self-confidence. A higher education administrator in
her early fifties, Brenda has crafted a self-presentation that attempts
to garner a level of respect that approximates what her white peers
are granted routinely by their staffs and colleagues.

And in reality, I'm certainly not as self-confident as most
people would probably think that I am, but that's what we
have to be. I can't exude a lack of confidence every time
I get ready to put my suit on in the morning and go to
work.... I feel like when I leave here in the morning, to go
to my job, that I'm supposed to know the answers.

Because Black and white women are "viewed differently" and "scrutinized differently," Brenda projects an attitude of knowing to offset ever-present perceptions of Black women as incapable and inferior. Appearing knowledgeable means that Brenda is "not very good at saying, 'I don't know.' Or, 'I'm not sure.' Or, anything that would lead someone that's working for me to think that I don't know what I'm doing." A constant vigilance accompanies her days, which she describes as requiring a "different energy level" focused on "always proving myself." She is exhausted by the pressure she feels to "compensate, and then *over*compensate, and then *re-over-*compensate, you know, on and on." She is also exasperated by the realization that her physical appearance carries an inordinate amount of sway over her coworkers. She thus stews in the knowledge that assessments of "my *clothing* should speak louder than what *I* have to say about things."

Within the elementary school where twenty-one-year-old Michelle is employed as an aide, the plantation resonances of mammification are disturbingly real and fitting: The master is the white male principal, the ladies are the white teachers, and the predominantly Black and Hispanic schoolchildren are the slaves. Each of the four Black women on staff is a paraprofessional, and Michelle painfully recognizes how they are "used" by the majority-white female faculty to deal with unruly schoolchildren. She feels that the larger-size Black women "look" the part of racial subordinate in the drama that the white men and women of the school uphold.

The faculty's perception of Michelle as a mammy blinds them to her relationship-building work and the logic of her approach to discipline. As a vexed Michelle says, "They don't ask. They just make assumptions. . . . They'll see that the kids will respect me, and then they automatically assume it's a Black thing. . . . So that's what I deal with." Mammification of her person dismisses the thought and labor involved in her "tactics" for relating to and disciplining the students. "Number one, I let the kids know, I love the kids, you know. And I'm always, constantly touching them, hugging them, you know. Trying to say, 'I've got love for you,' you know. And you build that relationship, that rapport with them that the teachers don't see."

With audible anger and frustration in her voice, Michelle correctly views the teachers as rendering her into a subordinate who is called in to "tak[e] care of their problems before I'm taking care of myself." Having to work amidst these assumptions is an experience Michelle likens to being asphyxiated:

> It's like if somebody's trying to put you in a box and put a lid over it, and only give you enough air to breathe, you know. Only move the lid to give you enough air to breathe, but not let people see who's in the box, type thing.... They're trying to intimidate you, but yet you're fighting to not be intimidated.

Kept alive for particular organizational needs, a mammy is never allowed to emerge or act of her own accord. People do not care to know who she is beyond the purposes to which she is put. Although describing her own mistreatment in dramatic terms, Michelle notes that her status is ameliorated by her pursuit of a college degree. She is shielded from the more "demean[ing treatment] beyond any level that you can even imagine" routinely shown to the three other Black women employees. Expected to feel grateful for their low-paying jobs, they are relatively defenseless against being "talked down to" and blamed for the misjudgments of higher-status individuals.

Ironically, yet understandably, these coworkers draw on a conceptualization of strength as endurance to focus not on the injustice of their work conditions, but on their shows of fortitude within them. As Michelle observes, their view of strength encourages them to say to themselves, "I deal with this on a daily basis, and yet I survive," as opposed to prompting them to challenge the legitimacy of the situation and conclude, "You know, I've dealt with this on a daily basis, and it's not right." The strength expected of such co-workers to comport themselves as mammies in the school, as well the strength that allows them to find validation under conditions of duress both hinge on their structural powerlessness. Remarking on how these Black women employees with virtually nonexistent authority are burdened with sole responsibility for low-status tasks, Michelle surmises that such women acquiesce to this role because it appears to bring rewards and avoid further sacrifice.

> You have to *lose* a lot of things in order to *fight*. But you gain *love*, you gain *affection*, you gain this, if you *don't* fight, and you just settle. You gain people coming to you, pattin' you on the back, you know. Maybe it's your boss man who's saying, "I really appreciate you staying late today. Although we couldn't, you know, pay you overtime."

But such recognition is distractive: As a tactic of mammification, it brings Black women no tangible rewards of power, choice, or respect in the workplace. Being strong is not a solution out of the quandary of such mistreatment and the lack of options outside the role of mammy. As Michelle painfully observes, "If you fight, you could die early. And if you *stay*, the way you are, you could still die early."

Protective Acts of Dissemblance

Learning over time that people are largely insensitive to them as fully human beings, some Black women learn to defensively keep their needs from view in order to avoid disappointment and hurt. Understandably, like Tasha, they fiercely commit to independence:

> You get tired of people telling you, "No," or they'll be there for you, and actually they're not. So what do you do? You rely on yourself, because you can't depend on nobody like

> you can depend on yourself.... It only took one or two
> people to tell me that they would be there for me, and they
> didn't, and you don't get but one chance. And so once you
> blow that one chance, and I know I'm the only one who
> can do it, then I only rely on me.

Such self-reliance is bound not only with doing for self, but with
not showing vulnerability. Although a widely used tool to manage
interactions within family and work situations, on occasion, the
intensity of Black women's performances surprises them. Celia
recounts being disturbed rather than flattered upon receiving a
letter from a friend eager to know, "How do you keep everything
together?":

> And when I read the letter, it freaked me out so bad, and I
> *never* could even respond to it. Because I was thinking, "It's
> all smoke and mirrors." I was thinking, you know, "This
> lady does not realize that, you know, *bad* things happen.
> Things can be falling down around me." And I was think-
> ing, "Do I *really* make people think that I am handling *ev-
> erything*," because, you know, inside you're going crazy.
> You're waking up in the middle of the night, you're freaked
> out, you're having all these problems. And I was just think-
> ing, "Am I ... that much of an actress that people believe
> that things are great, all the time?"

Celia expresses shock at the extent to which others are taken in by
her show of strength despite her subjective experiencing of in-
tense anxiety and even panic. However, she also discusses years of
extensive efforts to remain private and emotionally reserved, even
from persons she considers to be close friends:

> You have to kind of keep your cards close. You know, you
> may let people know a *little* bit, but you *never tell every-*

thing. Never.... I have like three *really close* friends, that I talk to on a regular basis.... But... if I told each one of them a story, and you asked each one of them, they're all going to have a different piece. I'm *never* going to tell *any* of them the whole thing. One of them will have a piece. Even if they put their three pieces together, it's still, there's still something missing. And I would *never do that* with anyone, would I tell them everything. *Never.*

Although Celia exhibits perhaps an extreme form of dissemblance, other women also speak of having trouble turning off the performance of strength. A program manager, thirty-nine-year-old Monique has erected a "wall" to shield herself from the comments and actions of coworkers who do not see her as a peer despite her superior performance and credentials. While seemingly necessary to survive her workplace, the walling of herself from others negatively impacts her intimate relationships.

I'm not very easy to *share* information. I even have to, um, work on that with my *husband*, because it's very hard to be a certain way all the [time] at work, and then come home and be this person that opens up and shares.... I have a problem of keeping a whole lot inside.... Weaknesses. Anything about us that could be perceived as a weakness.... To hurt us or... to *judge* us incorrectly.

Walls erected over time to manage threatening situations have a permanence not easily dismantled. Also drawing on the metaphor of a wall to describe her guardedness in all social situations, Yasmin, a thirty-two-year-old educator, movingly describes how her own barrier is a co-construction. Initially erected from the insensitivity of others, it is maintained through her own attempts at self-defense.

I feel like it's an action/reaction. You know, when I was a little girl, I went to private school. And in the whole school of 200 or so, there were five Black girls.... So, you know, people would say things. Like, I remember a boy once making monkey noises at me. Well, that's one brick in the wall. Or, you know, teachers coming by and wanting to touch the hair; that's brick number two. So, I think, *I* definitely *projected* [a wall], but it has come from a bunch of things over time.... And so people knew, very early on, not to cross a line with me, because otherwise I was gonna just blow up. And that was a way to keep people [away], you know. After a certain age, *nobody* said nasty, racist things to me, because they knew that they were going to get it if they did. And in order to sort of keep that up, it just requires this *insane* amount of energy.

Yasmin makes the salient point that while they may appear to be irrational, self-generated fortifications, the walls carried by Black women are protective structures laboriously built "brick by brick" in the face of ongoing mistreatment that chips away at their humanity.

The "*insane* amount of energy" required to manage daily affronts is echoed by Brenda, who speaks of the difficulty of switching from the independence she presents at work to a more interdependent mode of giving and receiving, caring and being cared for, at home.

It's, um, it's very, very, very, very, very, very hard for me to relax. It takes, um, it takes *a long time.* ... I find it hard to come *here* [home], and again, *alone*, and just shut that off.... I just have *me*, and this. And so, it's hard to turn that off. Um, but even if I *could*, and this probably has an impact on my ability to *have* a healthy relationship, because even if I had someone waiting here, to help me make the transition, I don't know that I have a lot to give. Because of the, um, what I do is really very emotionally exhausting. And so, um, it's hard for me to make the transition. It's hard for me to relax. . . .

Unable to give up the façade and acknowledge—that is, give room to—all that has been stifled and denied during her workday, Brenda suggests that being impassive is an attribute she has learned to present to the world in order to manage its traps and insensitivity to her needs. If Black women seem emotionless, these women are painfully aware of how they are in fact walled off from others by the litany of "assumptions" made about them, with regard to not being "interested in getting married" or "not interested in, um, having someone take out the garbage or, you know, all the other things that go along with having a partnership," explains Brenda.

Attributions of strength enable others to undertake a problematic detachment from the actual conditions of Black women's lives. As a result, Black women are left holding up more than their share of inequitable social situations. The anger, lack of approachability, and solitude often associated with strong Black women can be understood as reactions to the pervasive perception that they lack the sensitivities of others considered fully human. Moreover, the apparent depth and impenetrability of their walls reflect a long history of inadequate and hurtful interactions rather than these women's brazen refusal to be open to others.

Strength Becomes Us

To meet the demands placed on them to be strong, some Black women speak of developing a façade rather than completely identifying with the role. However, in their talk, evident is the immense difficulty they encounter as they try to maintain this distinction for themselves. As a case in point, Deidre, a twenty-five-year-old higher education administrator, uses the term "perceived strength" to describe her own posture of resilience. Although conceptually distinguishing between appearances and reality, when relating her own experiences, she begins in the first-person "I," moves to the culturally prescribed second-person "you," and finally speaks in the collective "we." Such shifts in pronoun convey the accommodations she and other Black women make to the dictates of strength:

> I might be stressing out about something or what have you, but you can't show other people that you're having a difficult time. And I don't know if that is a historical thing or just a societal type thing, that we're supposed to always be strong, and know the answers. And even though we are women, and women are supposed to have this feminine side where they can cry, I think as Black women we're not necessarily given that right as much, because we are also supposed to remain strong, for our families, and support our men, and in the workplace.

The "feminine" side that is attuned to and registers Black women's emotional needs is given little cultural or social standing. Consequently, those women committed to showing strength are also compelled to keep this aspect of their subjectivity far from public view and scrutiny. Forced to concede to pervasive expectations of their exceptionality, they must always "know the answers," "remain strong" for kin, male romantic partners, and coworkers, and forgo the "right" to acknowledge and express feelings and realities closely associated with white women.

The discourse of strength so shapes Black women's interactions with each other that few interviewees had ever seen their mothers cry—that is, outwardly reveal that they were anything but up to the tasks before them. Similarly, most of them hid their individual "weaknesses" from their own daughters and close women friends. Allene, a fifty-year-old administrative assistant, describes her elderly mom as still fiercely committed to a show of strength. Even among intimates, she "will cut you down before she lets you see her cry." Tasha recounts that growing up in a proud family of strong Black women, "we didn't see none of that stuff . . . the crying in the room, and the depression, and all of that stuff," despite the presence of profound emotional loads:

> TB: So you're saying that here you have your aunt who's raising three then four kids, right, more or less by herself. . . . And you know that she's working hard and she's trying, but you don't hear her [say]. . . .
> Tasha: You know, "Oh, I'm so tired. I can't go on." We don't hear that. We don't hear that. We don't hear, you know, "You all's going to have to get out and help," or, you know, "because I can't do this no more." And I don't recall anybody in my family ever saying that. We don't hear [long pause]. I don't recall ever hearing nothing like that from nobody [said in a barely audible voice].

Complaints and pleas for help are not statements Tasha remembers from her childhood. Such silences reflect not the absence of strains but the lack of conscious registering of the enormity of duress in Black women's lives.

Much is normalized by the circumstances of deprivation and expectations of their fortitude that Black women encounter. As Jennifer explains, "If *you* have dealt with problems all your life, and you've come to the point where that's *normal*, then it's *impossible* almost for you to pick out somebody else's similar situation and see that as a problem, if, in your eyes, it's just a normal life, every Black woman." Jennifer finds that her own family members look askance at women who cannot visibly embody confidence in their life choices.

Jennifer: At *either* side [of my family] . . . *you* gotta know what you're doing. [They believe that,] "You're, you're like, our roots or whatever or however. And, you know, [if] we don't have *you* to look to for guidance, how can you fall apart?"

TB: So you've got to keep up. . . .

Jennifer: Yeah. This façade. Yeah, I mean, even I, I find myself. And that *may be* something from them that I haven't *thought* about. I have a, I'm really, I'm *accused* a lot of being emotionless sometimes.

A "façade" is unresponsive to changing contexts, and allows Black women a singular response to all manner of experiences. In contemplating the effects of sporting a façade, Jennifer comes across a novel insight, "something from them that I haven't *thought* about": that she's inherited a particular stoicism that condemns the revelation of anxiety, confusion, or distress under any circumstances.

Say for instance you're in an office and someone fires you, you know, and some women would just break down and cry right there, you know—"I need my job. I'm feeding my kids." And me, I can't. I'd be like, "Whatever." And I may *leave*, and just break down in the corner in the closet by myself, but there's *something* that I guess I've been taught, and I, that's not a part of me.

What Jennifer emphasizes in her example are not the consequences of showing hurt and desperation (being ridiculed or treated unsympathetically), but the fact that public emotional release is "just not a part of me." Because of her exposure and accommodation to expectations of strength, she cordons off pain and worry from her conscious presentation of self. If these emotions are "just not a part of me," they have, at best, limited standing and value in her meaning-making. Such lack of emotion impacts her childrearing insofar as she has not cried in front of her daughter despite being "definitely" overwhelmed with "school, work, single mom, ugh."

> I don't think she's ever seen it. I really hadn't thought about that. I hadn't paid attention to that. I don't think *anybody's* ever seen it. I mean, I think maybe *one*, one of my girlfriends. . . . And it's not that I don't *say*, you know, that, "I'm going crazy. That [it] is driving me [crazy]," whatever, whatever. But as far as *showing* the emotion, I don't think people ever get to see that.

Jennifer's startling realization about her stoicism suggests that she has unconsciously operated by a set of rules that, while not necessarily explicit, do not lack any of the force of overt prescription. Given such terms of limited expression, understandably yet meaningfully, Jennifer likens the expectations of strength to "a Black Jesus girl thing":

> So, I'm supposed to figure it out, and *really* that's what I've been doing. I've been *forcing* myself to figure out how I'm doing what I'm doing. Because *people expect me to be this person*, you know, I'm not. If I was to, say, for instance, lose my apartment, or if I was to lose my car, or my lights went out, my people would freak out. Because that's not supposed to [happen]. I'm *too strong* for that. And, you know, I have this, all this *power* to make things different. And I'm not supposed to suffer like other people.

Expecting Black women to "*be this* person, you know, I'm not," strength discursively renders Jennifer into a transcendent savior rather than the multidimensional, developing, and sensitive human being she is. She therefore cannot be forthcoming about her needs and the exigencies of her life as a single working mother completing her undergraduate studies. Rather, she is pressured to present herself to friends and intimates—"my people"—as impervious to the actual worries she experiences because in the world of their reputed strength, Black women are "not supposed to suffer like other people." And if she does suffer and struggle, Jennifer finds that her family and friends typically respond to her strength-discrepant behaviors with statements such as, "What the hell is wrong with you?" and outright rejections of her feelings of being overwhelmed or in need of support. Consequently, to keep up the appearance of her strength, she engages in an unseen but laborious process of "*forcing* myself to figure out how I'm doing what I'm doing."[4]

Conclusion

The constant association of Black women with strength comes from the extent of the consensus—within families, communities, and society—that it is the one social role that Black women should play well and faithfully. It arises not out of Black women's innate or essential qualities but from persistent demands placed on them to be included in an American social drama primarily as the stock character of the selfless, stoic, silent, and therefore "strong" Black woman. By taking on the needs of others as her own, in having to define herself by the extent to which others are made secure by her efforts, a strong Black woman, Aisha notes, "covers *everything*. She's expected to *cover everything*." For those who look to Black women for emotional and material support, strength is a "sincere fiction" (Vera, Feagin, and Gordon 1995) that strategically disregards the reality of their exploitation. Consequently, the strongest women are also expected to give the most of themselves to others, and a sizable power over Black women accrues to those who invoke their strength. As Angie observes, references to a Black woman's strength are rarely above suspicion and often are duplicitous:

"And when people say you're strong because you're working three jobs, and you take care of this house and you take care of that house, sometimes those are the people, that's making that comment, who are the ones that you're helping." Using the moral judgment of strength to compel them to concede to unfair relational demands, expectations of strength pave the way for the disempowerment of Black women.

Much of the labor extracted from such strong women is gendered in that they are obligated to carry the responsibility of nurturing others, to be "the titty of the world," as Nita observes. In line with its justification of inequities, the controlling image of strength asserts that a weak Black woman either buckles under life and its nonnegotiable caregiving pressures, or is unacceptably focused on her own needs. Self-knowledge and an examination of one's life as a multidimensional human being are not part of the experience of being strong. Such activities are immediately characterized by the discourse as inappropriately taking time and energy away from a Black woman being of use to others. The emphasis on taking care of others is reinforced, within the subjectivity of Black women, by an internalized concern that they not be viewed as selfish by those around them. The logic of the strength discourse, then, largely eclipses the existence of an experience-based rather than discourse-driven standpoint.

Generated by the discourse of strength is a language of praise and a semblance of power that are not borne out in an examination of Black women's lives. Because of its fundamental view of Black women as laborers for others, adhering to strength's prescriptions renders much of Black women's experiences hidden to others and themselves. The distinctiveness that strength claims of Black women consistently deflects attention away from the vulnerabilities and needs they share with other human beings. As Alexis, a twenty-three-year-old single mother explains, being called and treated by coworkers and supervisors as a strong Black woman is a way of saying "you're different," which contradicts her own subjective sense of being "just like everyone else. . . . I have the same fears and hurts and pains just like everyone else." While strength highlights Black women's reputedly limitless ability to endure and care, it does so while mystifying and denying the toll of such demands on their psyches, bodies, and relationships. Consequently, showing strength necessitates the creation of an extensive psychological backstage that leaves much of the texture and nuance of Black women's existence out of view. However, despite being defined as so caring, concerned, and other-directed that "everybody in your family relies on you," some women, like Dana, a married librarian and mother, do privately wonder "What does that do to you in the long run?" It is this mismatch between façade and reality that becomes embodied as physical and psychological distress, a process that is the focus of Chapter 4.

4 / Lies Make Us Sick

Embodied Distress Among
Strong Black Women

> I thought my grandparents was the *best*. I think my mom is the *best*, because I knew they could deal with it. But then, I'm like, really now? Are they actually really dealing with it, you know? Because look at that, they got all these illnesses, and I think all that adds to the weight and illnesses. The *emotional* part. [They] never cried. We never had much crying in our family. If you cried [the response was], "What's wrong with you?"
>
> —Traci

> What I see in a lot of Black women here is, "Alright, since I can't have money or people, I can't live up to somebody's standards," or something in their life is not right, that food becomes a way for them to, it becomes the emotional outlet.
>
> —Aisha

To naturalize patterns of social disenfranchisement, strength is deployed to tell lies about Black women. Higher-status race–gender groups utilize it in the hopes that it becomes not simply a performance, but an identity. The use of strength imposes a definition of who Black women are, or at least who they should aspire to be in order to gain acceptance from others and secure a foothold in the social world. Psychologically intrusive, the discourse of strength renders the material and relational aspects of oppression into realities Black women should endure rather than injustices worthy of their outrage and challenge. To the extent that this is accomplished, the discourse promotes the apparent reality of "strong Black women" whose "inborn" qualities make talk of female oppression within racism conceptually untenable. Steeped in the discourse of strength, members of society perceive and evaluate Black women on how well they seem to be managing their responsibilities—that is, on what they do. And in response, Black women invested in being recognized as good, moral, and "strong" tend to edit personal needs and perspectives from their discourse-driven interactions and careful self-presentations. However, as suggested in the previous chapter, Black women provide clues that strength is anything but a natural identity.

Notably, several women used the term "internalization" to name the many ways in which they and others meet expectations. By not letting "those feelings *out* to anybody," such women turn to their bodies to "absorb" injustices and maintain their reactions "all bottled inside." Internalization strategies suppress a growing sense that the demands and all the display rules that attend to being perceived as a strong Black woman are unjust. As a result, internalization techniques—such as increasing their workloads to take on obligations that others have cast off or failed to honor, or engaging in compensatory behaviors such as excesses in eating, drinking, or shopping—do not encourage outright critiques of the strength discourse. Rather, such practices cover over realities—the inequitable demands made of Black women, and how they really feel about such expectations—in order to protect the idea of strength. In adopting internalization strategies, then, Black women demonstrate their allegiance to the discourse and its success in convincing them of its moral authority to reign over what they feel, despite the intensity of their discrepant emotions. As a result, women who rely on internalization are also bound by the belief that anything other than persuasive shows of strength "becomes a flaw in who we are," rather than a reflection of problematic social conditions in their lives. In this way, internalization is a costly form of self-silencing, which can become embodied as physical and psychological distress.

Fed Up

A commitment to the discourse of strength compels Black women to express a range of realities obliquely, often through eating practices. Choosing strength over self, overeaters assuage hurts with food rather than overtly critiquing the relational and ideological conditions of their existence among others. Although many women share Deidre's view that culturally food is "the cure-all for anything," others like Brenda additionally note that overeating is simply the most visible and perhaps common of several "*excesses* that we have. Excesses of drinking . . . even getting involved with like abusive relationships. . . . Not only weight, but a lot of the issues that I think we have. You know, *overspending*, different things like that. . . . Everyone does different things to feel better." Compensatory internalization strategies in Brenda's family include her mother's chain smoking, her sister's extensive outlays for beautification and fashion, and her own use of alcohol to relax. Connecting these behaviors to the demands placed on herself and her kin as women perceived to be stalwart supports, she wonders "facetiously . . . if the reason we don't need to take . . . a little pink pill, or we're *not* taking them is because we find *other ways* to medicate ourselves." As Brenda's examples suggest, overeating and other compensatory behaviors allow Black women to stave off the direct expression of emotions that would call much of their social worlds into question.

In discussing her gain and eventual loss of sixty pounds, Traci emphasizes that the most significant influence on her eating was her "confus[ion]" regarding matters in her life. She draws connections between being strong, years when she "kind of kept things inside and dealt with them," and finding a temporary "exit" in eating.

> TB: So, why does the eating begin?
>
> Traci: I think you have to have, to *me*, it's something going on. You just, whatever. You just say, "Life goes any kind of way." You don't really *care*. . . . Because I know after that, I just really didn't think about nothing. You don't, you're not focused on anything, you're not going anywhere. You just sit there and you're at a standstill. "Well, what am I going to do?" "I don't know." "You don't know?" You know, you just. You don't know. You're, probably you're *confused*. You *eat*. It's an exit. You eat. . . . At that time, it's an outlet. It works for you. You don't have to deal with anybody, because you just put food in your mouth. . . . At the time, it was my peace. It was my outlet. . . . You don't even taste the food.

When she was eating compulsively, Traci was dealing with an unsatisfying marriage, raising a daughter and a nephew, working in a low-wage job as a nursing home assistant, and managing the health of a mother with a formidable succession of weight-related illnesses—diabetes, congestive heart failure, stroke, high blood pressure, thyroid problems, and kidney failure. Contrary to her performance of the strength she was raised to "pick up," Traci was troubled in her life. Recalling this period, she expresses feelings of entrapment and uncertainty evident in her metaphor of being "at a standstill." While falling short of prompting changes in her marriage and work, her eating allowed her a temporary "exit" and release: "It was my peace. It was my outlet."

Arguably, the respite came not only from the repetitive action of ingesting food, but also from the internal conversation that accompanied her eating. Holding a mental dialogue with herself,

Traci was able to voice and indirectly recognize those realities not allowed open expression in the performance of strength—"Well, what am I going to do?' 'I don't know.' 'You don't know?'" Such exchange is distinct from the strength discourse in two ways—first, it is devoid of mandating shoulds invested in suppressing these realities to the discourse; second, it focuses on gaining insight into Traci's actual experiences—that is, what she knows and needs in spite of the prescriptions attendant on being a strong Black woman.

As does Traci, Jennifer views the eating of the strong and large women in her family as allowing them what strength does not—time away from "the struggles of life. You know, the one time in the world they have to rest is, 'Hey, eat.' One thing they know they can do well is eat and that's their quiet time. You eat and you relax, you know." The outlet of eating is particularly necessary for women who lack coping skills or supportive relationships through which to process the difficulties in their lives.

Angie reflects on how the injunction that women will care for family left her mother with no recourse to take constructive action against being taken advantage of in such relationships:

> You don't have no way to vent *your anger. Your frustrations.* When these bills are not, don't seem to balance out, who do you fuss, you know, go to, vent to? And my mom had *no* friends. All of her friends were like, you know, they were doing their own thing, and they would tell her, "Stop paying all up in there." And that's their only advice. She didn't have anyone she could go to and say, "Girl, just listen. Don't calm me; just let me vent." She didn't have nobody like that. And, it builds up on you. And then the weight builds up. You've got, with stresses, you're going to have heart disease, you're going to have this and that. It's not like just you're dealing with heavy weight. You're dealing with confusions in your life.

Such "stresses" and "confusions" are vitally tied to the relational inequities that pervade the lives of strong Black women. Rather than support for her discontent, Angie's mother received platitudes and dismissals of her dilemma. Neither allowed her what she needed—an opportunity to voice, think through, and evaluate the meaning of her emotions. This lack of honest, nonjudgmental dialogue pushed her further into a "confusion" surrounding the management of her needs amidst those of family members. Angie adds that beyond general advice, her mother required assistance to see and step outside of the discourse of strength: to realize that some of this struggle and the "mak[ing] our lives hard on ourselves" is generated not simply by external demands but also by not realizing that "it's times when we need to say, 'No. Can't do it.'" Unable to examine her life beyond the self-silencing and self-denial of strength, a woman can find that weight "builds up on you." That is, bottled-up emotions weigh down the mind and body in the absence of open, clarifying talk.

Living in a rural southern community in which, she estimates, "95 percent" of the women are "severely obese," Rita believes that some of the metaphorical and scripted religious maxims encourage the use of internalization strategies. She contends that a majority of these women lack a direct language for speaking about "what's really important . . . about issues of the heart."

It's more like being caught up in the rhetoric of the religion. So they can quote you the Bible. They sing and they dance in church, and going to church is important. But, when it comes down to it, I'm not so sure like they've addressed what's really eating at them. . . . I'm not saying that what they're feeling is not true. But you can't use that as an excuse and not deal with reality. And the reality of it is that the majority of them and *me* are doing it all.

Like the overeating, Rita views the encouraging religious phrases as having limited value. Although these words acknowledge that "something in their life is not right," they also limit the extent to which problems of self and community are allowed to surface and be faced. In particular, Rita questions cultural norms that expect women to be "doing it all" (see Weems 2004). She observes that the women "are not laying their burdens down by the riverside. Because if they were ... they would really be light and carefree and ready to *tackle* things," rather than being "just bogged down" in their bodies and minds by these circumstances.

For many Black women, their overeating is associated with experiencing anger that they can no longer deny or maintain behind their walls. Within a focus group, college students Kira and Macy disclose the emotional logic of their eating.

> Kira: I feel like food is the easiest thing to get to, you know.... Let's say I'm having trouble, problems with people in general. Like, I go to work, I go to school every day, and people are always interrogating me or whatever. And it's like, "Well, right now, food will solve the problem. It'll satisfy me." You know, it's the easiest thing to get to.
>
> Macy: Shuts you up [said almost inaudibly].
>
> TB: What did you say?
>
> Macy: Shuts you up for a second.
>
> TB: Well, if we didn't, if you weren't "shut up for a second," what might happen?
>
> Macy: You would explode. You would just start telling people off, and wouldn't care if you hurt anybody's feelings.... I always keep stuff *in*, and I'll let it stick to me. And if you hold stuff in, it's going to eat away at you. Just like food, [it] will eat away at you, if you hold it in.

As an activity, eating enables Black women to register and attend to some of their needs without disrupting the fiction of their strength. When Macy uses food to "shu[t] you up," she does so to keep from "exploding," that is revealing the emotions she experiences but which a good Black woman cannot show. More critical and fundamental than the fact of her eating is the use of her body to absorb rather than vent emotions and critiques of the social relations she finds unjust. The attendant weight gain she and other women experience can be understood, both as a kind of release and as a problematic reabsorption of feelings within the economy of their bodies.

In the following personal example, Michelle implicates the mammification she experiences at work in her overeating:

> And let's say that you're in the [teachers'] lounge or something, and you're eating amongst white people. You're *ticked off* at what just happened, you know. . . . So, okay, I went to [a donut store], and instead of getting two donuts, I got *six* donuts. And I'm eating them one after *the other.* And I have donut holes, and then my *lunch*, and then *ice cream.* So, white people will look at you, or any other type of race who *don't* understand what you're going through, will look at you and go, "What the hell's her problem? Why are you eating?" . . . But they don't ask [you], "What's wrong?" . . . They would just assume, "Well, she's just like an overeater or something. That's why she's big. That's why."

In the internal monologue that accompanies her consumption of a succession of food, Michelle importantly acknowledges "what you're going through"—that her colleagues are exploiting her as a person of lower social standing and limited power. Although eating is socially safe, it is ultimately a flawed outlet for growing wells of frustration.

Recently diagnosed by her physician as clinically obese and in need of losing 100 pounds, Michelle discusses her overeating—"because I know I'm not hungry and I'm eating this"—as a long-standing coping mechanism for her anger that she feels prohibited from expressing.

> I've even found myself, like, when I was talking about [the TV sitcom] *The Parkers* [abbreviated chuckle], and how Nikki was just eating down in that bag of chips. And I know that has been me at some times. You know, if I'm really ticked off about something, I'll either do one of three things. But really one of *two*. The *last* choice I'll do is clean something. The second to last choice I'll do is cut my hair [nervous voice]. The first thing I'll do is eat, and I'll just like go in there. And I've gotten, I've *kind* of gotten away from that. . . . But I'd say, the last time I've *really, really* done that, like on a habitual basis, [was] like when I was a sophomore in high school. But now it's like, things get to me, but, I don't know. If I don't have what I want by me, then I won't eat it. And, or I'll just shrug it off, and repress it, and just move on.

Within this description of her options for managing affronts to her person, Michelle reveals that she would resort to food "on a habitual basis." She also remarks that she has only recently moved away from that alternative. However, her replacement strategy for eating—"I'll just shrug it off, and repress it, and just move on"—seems equally problematic. Rather than attending to her anger and the contexts that give rise to it, such repression denies and disregards it. Michelle is not moved any closer to confronting the person and remedying the situation that has violated her needs and expectations. Once again, her body is called upon to cover for such unfairness.

Overeating reflects strong Black women's limited outlets for voicing a range of human emotions. Explains Michelle, as a strong

Black woman, one must "not be seen coping, basically." And yet, as a human, "you *do*, we *have* to cope, we *have* to cope with whatever we do." In a similar vein, Angie challenges a common logic that focuses on excess weight as the source of ill health. Instead, she identifies the strains in women's lives and their lack of coping skills as the often hidden but very critical causes of both the over-eating and the physical ailments that ensue. She argues, "It's not because we overweight that we got heart problems, and heart fail-ures, and high blood pressure. It's 'cause we *stressed* out! And we don't know how to *vent* it the right way. Or, if we vent it, we vent it with a Häagen-Dazs ice cream or some other ice cream."

Black women are pressured to manage both stressors and their stress responses on their own. Their eating reflects the discourse-driven insistence that Sheila, a college educator, knows well: "It's *again* we're supposed to *suck it all up* and *be there* for our Black community, for our Black men, be the foundation of the Black church, etc., etc. But you do it all in *silence, nameless*, with no credit given and no appreciation of *anything* that we do. . . . *That* takes a toll, that kind of stress, and that kind [of] 'Mum's the word.'"

Venting through eating is inadequate, not simply because a woman's anger is not voiced directly to others, but also because overweight on Black women is often viewed as a physical marker of their strength or their ability to endure (Baturka, Hornsby, and Schorling 2000; Hebl and Heatherton 1997; Townsend Gilkes 2001). As Jennifer notes, strength saddles Black women with be-havioral and physical expectations: that as women they are sup-posed to "take care of [their] people. All the time. Always. Food, clothes, husband, iron, wash"; and that weight gain is not serious because "they're *Black* and they're *supposed to be* big like that." As a result, the messages being sent through eating and weight gain ironically feed into the construction of Black women as operating with distinct emotional and physical capacities.

Across socioeconomic statuses, Black women faced with strength demands struggle to take their bodies seriously. Like other self concerns, physical and emotional wellness retreats to the background of a strong Black woman's daily interactions. Without such acknowledgment, Black women often shy away from facing "what they've let themselves grow into," which are the expectations they have been raised to pick up from childhood regarding their strength. Understandably, Aisha observes, some distressed and overweight Black women will "*overcompensate* in other areas" by cooking for children, buying them items, or remaining in abusive heterosexual relationships.

> And I think to a certain extent, overweight Black women *play* into that, also. You know, "Yeah, I may be overweight, but baby, I can cook!" And stuff like that.... Even though you know you're overweight, and you might not even be *comfortable* with it, you just *keep pushing it further and further* down inside of you, because you have so many *other* things that you're trying to deal with.

To "deal with" the body would require facing the self and a life that a woman might find unsatisfying, draining, and fundamentally unfair. In the absence of confronting her deep feelings, those she carefully hides from view, being strong is a familiar way of managing these uncomfortable realizations. Her attending to others to the exclusion of listening to and caring for herself accomplishes the work of pushing such discomfort "*further and further* down inside of you," to the point that it is detached from a woman's conscious awareness.

Speaking about a woman she knows, whose overweight now has impending fatal consequences, Tasha invokes the phrase "let[ting] herself go." Typically a condemnation of women who fail to take adequate steps to guard against stigmatized weight gain, the phrase seems to have a more profound significance in this example. As Tasha describes, this woman is "unhealthy ... sick" and has been told by her doctor "that if she doesn't lose fifty pounds, she is going to die." The fact that she has not made dietary and lifestyle changes strikes Tasha as a form of suicide: "Why do you have to kill yourself, when there's plenty [of] other outside things that'll do it, you know?" Although critical of this woman's current health practices, Tasha speaks of the admiration she has for her strength.

> She raised her two girls and her son by herself.... Actually, she's a woman who encourages me. So, you know, I mean, she knows about everything that happened in the family 'cause she's somebody who I could go and talk to, and she encourages me that, you know, "Don't let that discourage you," you know. "Keep on going," and everything like that. But I wouldn't, if I *disqualified* her as a [strong] woman, it would be because of what she is letting *herself* go through. Not because of what she does for her family. Because she's still there for them and all of that, but, I mean, I would want her to do better by *herself.*

The weight that this woman has gained in recent years reflects to Tasha that something is amiss in her life. "Do[ing] better by *herself*" would entail following the advice of her doctor and making her health a priority.

Arguably what Tasha does not consider is that compliance with the doctor's orders is a challenge for any strong Black woman. It requires the recognition that she has a self outside of her responsibilities to others. What such a woman knows too well is how to put more stock in the image of her strength than in her own emotional reality. Suggesting a similar difficulty in transitioning from being strong to demonstrating self-concern, Macy relates the example of a great-grandmother who raised generations of biological and community children and "never took time out for herself." She remained silent about her stomach cancer "until she just, just, it was like, like right at the end, when they couldn't do nothing." These women seem to have let themselves go in the sense that there is very little, if any, voice left with which to contest the demands of strength. With regard to physical health, the concern we develop from a sensitivity to the discourse of strength is that the weight-related diseases that plague the Black female community may be embodied manifestations of the contradictory distinction of being strong and a "second-class citizen," even in one's own estimation (Joseph 1981, 92).

Locked Bodies

Although anger is the most common emotion associated with Black women's compulsive eating, vulnerability resulting from violation is also a significant contributor. Abuse survivors speak of resorting to eating to retreat from relationships in which their safety was not guaranteed (Thompson 1994). In the wake of sexual abuse, overeating and subsequent weight gain can be purposeful tools for shielding the body from future harm. In the words of Yasmin,

> I will not go into detail, but I am an abuse survivor. I think a lot of women, who were taught that you should not have sex before marriage, are *hiding* the sexy. And I think there's a whole culture, and a whole way of *covering up with fat*, things that you are not supposed to be using. . . . Sexual abuse is a big problem in the Black community. If *you* had somebody hurt your physical body, the one thing you're going to do, or you're *not* going to do, is sort of let it all out. . . . And I think there are a lot of obese women who are basically hiding their bodies.

Yasmin recalls periods during her adolescence of engaging in "disordered, binge eating. Just out of stress, you know, where I took a fifteen-minute period" to ingest food. Her weight gain was an intentional way of "lock[ing]" her body up so that neither she nor anyone could use it and expose her to further abuse. And yet when her emotional disconnection became a concern to her mother, she staunchly, at age 15, invoked her strength as an innate quality incompatible with the reality of her victimization and hurt: "My mother said, 'That's it. You're going to see a doctor.' And then I cried, 'Black people don't go see therapists.' "

Remarking on the existence of violence in the lives of women she knows, Tamika, a forty-year-old public health officer, also sees that "weight is a cover for some deeper issues" which a woman either "hasn't dealt with" or that others are not willing to acknowledge:

> You know, it's easier to talk about weight than to talk about, you know, "I'm in an abusive relationship." Because people can accept and be comfortable talking to you about weight, but when you talk about, you know, "My husband's beating me every day," people are going to *push away* from you.

Eating offers solace "when, you know, like the world is crashing down around you, you can make some *dressing*, some *greens*, and feel pretty good," observes Jennifer. It can also provide emotional and physical "layers of protection" to hide the self. So while, Tamika observes, "on the *outside* [a woman's world] is perfect," inside it may be "just *shattered*" and "coming down, coming down, coming down." Strong women are habituated to a familiar pattern in which "you're *raised* that way. You know, you *keep* everything. Everything.... It's just like, you just *internalize everything.*" It is such absorption and hiding of issues that has led Tamika to her own "chronic illnesses," such as "*stomach* problems out the waz[oo] [chuckle] ... because I have internalized *all* the stress, all the feelings, you know, from *childhood.*" For these women, the weight they carry is a proxy for the extent of violation and ongoing vulnerability they experience. As Yasmin asserts, in "shedding layers" one "sheds protection." Thus, to lose weight would be to give up defenses that have served such women well in unpredictable and hurtful circumstances.

Lost in the Act: Black Women's Depression

Despite the documented reluctance of Black women to associate themselves with depression, telling yet most often brief discussions of depressive experiences were not uncommon in the interviews. What the women considered to be clinical depression—states in which a woman was worn down by her struggles, had nothing left, was suicidal, had a "breakdown" (Clark Amankwaa 2005)—was readily evident among the women of their families and communities. When relating their understanding of depression, the women's tones shifted noticeably to a lower register, sometimes rendering their words barely audible. Depression talk was less animated and more contemplative than other discussions of strength, as though it were part of a very private level of feeling that rarely was put into words.

When Black women discuss depression, they convey states of existence saturated with palpable exhaustion, anger, and regrets. They speak of "burnout," "drowning," and needing to "take off the mask, and just kind of breathe a little bit." A graphic artist in her early thirties, Milly speaks about the reality of depression among the women in her family:

[Despite appearances], a lot of women are sad with their situation. Because they don't speak up.... If you're consistently trying to meet the needs of everybody, and *not* meeting the needs for yourself, I think that over time, it builds up a lot of anxiety and just *overwhelming feeling*. And so, I think that's where depression comes from. It's not being able to do *everything* that you need to do right when you want to do them.

Accessing and discussing this depth of feeling is difficult for strong Black women. Exclaims Jennifer, "We *don't exist!* We are *numb to ourselves* because we've had to put on this *role* for so long. That's why *Black* women *gossip* so doggone much. Because *they,* talking about *me,* oh no! Let's talk about *her* or *you!* We don't, we don't exist. The world has not made us into its existence." The lack of talk about self is reflective of the problem of not being perceived as human, with a range of qualities worth recognizing and discussing. Jennifer reads the bravado, Black women's voiced lack of concern regarding their psyches, as "ways for us to help put the hurt down."

Black women do not generally see depressive episodes as occasioned by brain chemistry or genetic predisposition. They focus attention on the intensity and persistence of the hardships in their lives toward which they are allowed no outrage or direct expression. In discussing the effect of constant struggle on the psyche, Jennifer provides the example of her grandmother who long "bit her tongue." In her old age, however, this woman is now speaking out and "tellin' them where they can go with a lot things." This "obnoxious" behavior follows years spent as a domestic enduring the words and disparaging actions of white employers while returning home to a violent husband.

> You know, your job abuses you, you're slavin', you're takin' care of people's kids, you know. Somebody else's house. They're an alcoholic. They talk *to you* crazy, but you need the money because you're got seven kids at home. And then you come home and your husband's beatin' your butt, and you know. . . . That's a lot.

Jennifer sees her grandmother's depression as the accumulation of unfairness and inequity woven into her life. Despite "fighting against the *odds*" and trying to play by the rules set for her at home and at work, a woman can find herself always expected to settle for less than she deserves. Her achievements and recognition are still not what they should be, with little acknowledgment of the powerlessness and abuse she has endured in both family and work settings. Depression is as Pamela, a self-employed stylist in her late thirties, describes a "bottoming out, when you've just had enough" of being abused and hurt.

Although tying together her grandmother's long-term mistreatment to a depression stewing within her over time, Jennifer insists that among the women in their family, the concept of "depression is not even a part of their conversation." For them, depression is akin to a psychotic state, evident in "something *drastic.* . . . When you talk about depression, they want to see you cuttin' your wrists and trying to jump out of the window [chuckle], you know. . . . [T]o them, *every woman* had, every Black woman has problems."

For other women, depression is conceptualized as something from which Black women are protected. If they are strong enough to handle life, they are capable of avoiding depression. Tasha draws on two voices to express her ambivalence toward acknowledging a state of pain, confusion, and introspection that is so at odds with how Black women are supposed to exist in the world.

I think they are a lot less *depressed* than white women, because we *know* struggle. *We* know, you know, what it is to make it or whatever. So, it's easier for us to *accept* when we don't get a job or when we don't get a raise or whatever, versus Buffy, you know, who has had everything, you know. . . . I think that it would be *good* if more Black people *seek* counseling or whatever, just to, you know, make them feel not as *worthless*, but not because of *depression*. Because I don't think we are a depressed people.

Despite her proud assertions of the invulnerability of Black people to depression, Tasha describes a period in her life of great weariness, an experience that resulted from "struggl[ing] too much" and having no one to turn to for assistance or emotional support.

> You don't see what my godmom calls "the light at the end of the tunnel." Then, I mean, you give up. And, you don't want to do. I mean, you get tired. Because actually, to tell you the truth, I've, I've done that. I mean, it's been several occasions where I'm just, I'm *tired*. I'm just tired. . . . You're *tired*, and you can get so tired and struggle and give up and literally die. From depression or whatever, because you can't see no end. There is no way out. Because, every day, something happens. Every day is something new and you, I mean, you just cannot take any more.

In a rare moment of self-revelation—"actually, to tell you the truth"—Tasha personalizes the account of depressive symptoms that she originally introduces in the second-person voice. She emphasizes, however, that such self-disclosure is uncommon in her interactions with family because of her commitment to appearing steadfast:

> They don't see me. I don't let nobody see. . . . They won't know until I've come through. . . . But, *me* going through it, you will never know it. Uh nuh. I just, 'cause I, I'm a *firm* [believer that] I've just got to handle it myself.

Although she sees potential value in counseling ("we didn't grow up, you know, thinking, you know, that thing about therapists are not good for, you know, Black people"), Tasha is more committed to being a proud upholder of strength in her *"God-fearing* family . . . [in which] *to this day*, none of them have never been to a therapist." Taken together, the assertions and recantations in

Tasha's narrative suggest that rather than protect Black women from depression, the strength discourse shelters them from self-scrutiny and the searching gaze of others that might reveal their less than optimal functioning and profound needs for loads not so burdensome.

Breakdowns: The Underside of Strength

Several interviewees noted the prevalence of "breakdowns" among the strong Black women they knew and admired. As sudden and dramatic periods of retreat from their responsibilities to others, breakdowns took the form of leaving home for hours or days, staying in bed, committing suicide, and dying in one's sleep. Usually talk of these collapses emerged deep in the interviews and these crises were noted without much affect. As Sheila explains, the imperative to do the work of family and community with little acknowledgment results in an "angry bitterness," which is the foundation of depressive episodes.

> I think it comes out in the nervous breakdown. You know, they talk about Black men going crazy. *That's* the most paid attention to. There are Black women who go crazy too.... I think it happens with *drugs and crack cocaine,* and mothers who prostitute their kids.... I think *that's* what it looks like and it's ugly. Women who walk off and leave their kids in the house for days on end.... White women do some of the same things, but I think for different reasons. And *perceived* in much different ways. You know, a Black woman who does all this, she's just a ghetto animal.

Physical health is also compromised by such repressed anger. As Sheila continues, "There's diabetes, cancer, breast cancer, the high incidence of it. Higher incidence of all these health disorders that are going on with Black women, and how quickly we die, too."

Depressive episodes or "breakdowns" are a hidden cost of strength, a "hush-hush" reality that strong women tend to shield from view. Sheila describes her mother as a *"consummate hostess and a sort of perfectionist,"* as well as a master of dissemblance: "You know, she *maintains* a certain kind of decorum, and a certain kind of *outward togetherness.* Even if *inside,* she's conflicted or she's having a nervous breakdown or she's depressed or anxious or whatever, because my mother never sort of. She's the type who *we* see her sweat, but nobody else knows." In a matter-of-fact manner, Sheila states that she is heir to a particular legacy: "Because my mother has had a nervous breakdown. My grandmother had one before her, and I think her mother had one before her." While perhaps referring to an inherited biochemical proclivity, Sheila also clearly acknowledges the existence of an intergenerational mandate of strength to which all these women have adhered. Rita describes a similar pattern of silences when speaking of the unacknowledged history of "breakdowns" among the strong women of her family.

> And when I say breakdown, particularly the *minor* breakdown, I mean just leaving the house, not being seen for a couple of days.... You know, this family certainly has a history of mental illness.... And when I look at the Black women, you know, I can *always* remember, the Black women that I know, that I *really* consider strong, have really had these breakdowns.... Like too much metallic stuff clings to their body. And really they just needed to go cry. Or, I don't know, drink, smoke, whatever they need to do, to get it off. You know, to like pry some of it off.

The breakdowns described are not the result of an overwhelming life change but of the accrual of baggage that buries the self and requires a drastic act of shutting down in order to allow the woman to reemerge. They demonstrate the inability of the body and mind to contain indefinitely the demands that are placed on "strong" women. As such, breakdowns serve a homeostatic function because the release of emotion during a breakdown allows the woman to express what being strong does not—fatigue, frustration, and a refusal to carry on.

However, akin to the internalization strategies of eating, shopping, or drinking, depression's temporary exits and withdrawals also tend to maintain rather than contest the ruse of strength. That is, they do not typically result in more realistic and self-focused guides for Black women's behavior. Like Rita's mother and Sheila's women kin, most strong Black women return to the same expectations and social relations that prompted the breakdown. The potential for change and critique is diminished because too few people, the women included, view depressive experiences as part of the public story of their womanhood. Since these episodes are not integrated into the shared memories of strength, Black women are not encouraged to investigate the role and its costs.

Despite this lack of acknowledgment, depressive episodes elicit knowing sympathy among Black women, particularly with regard to those kin and friends they love and admire. Such are viewed not as weak or bad women, but as human beings overwhelmed, as fifty-seven-year-old Yvonne notes, with "so many trials and tribulations that they just cannot deal." Furthermore, when discussed, there is little surprise or outrage about these periods of distress. However, what is rare is a conscious and critical tying of strength to depression, or an evaluation of strength in light of its toll on women's psyches and bodies. In other words, breakdowns are not conceptually incorporated into the view of Black women as strong nor is their occurrence used to question the construction of strength or Black women's commitments to this discourse.

Struggling to Come to Terms
with Depression

While only a few women spoke directly and personally about depression, most others noted in passing periods of physical and emotional crisis that could have been depressive episodes. Among her peers in their mid-twenties, Kiki sees "depression, *big time* [as well as] denial. A lot of denial. Denial about who you are. Denial of what *you're* capable of." As with other women who discussed depression within the Black community, Kiki's evocative imagery about the distress strongly suggests that she was speaking from personal experience, despite her use of more oblique third- and second-person voices:

> A lot of these women are feeling these odd feelings, and they just kind of override them. They don't even pay attention to them. . . . I think they know, deep down inside, that they're incapable of just, day by day doing all this, and that one day, the egg is going to crack, you know. And the ball is going to drop, but they don't want to come to terms with that. . . . You revert to drinking or smoking or screaming or yelling, or, you know, other things to kind of cover up what really is going on inside. . . . The depression just grows and grows.

The "denial" of one's subjectivity, of "what really is going on inside," emerges from ongoing self-deception. Because such denial does not directly or adequately deal with the demands placed on Black women, the "depression just grows and grows" beneath a woman's efforts to feel better and keep up a convincing portrayal of herself as strong. A returning college student, Soraya speaks of her stifled frustration as "a time bomb waiting to go off," and Marie expresses concern about a similar erosion that she terms "letting [yourself] go by not taking care of yourself *emotionally, spiri-*

tually, professionally." This lack of self-care often implicates the family norms that "put all the work on the females," a common practice that few could change or directly challenge without incurring the disapproval of others.

Rita clearly connects her clinical depression to the same cultural expectations of enduring struggle and extensive caretaking that others noted. Although quite angry and voiceful about such demands, she was markedly ambivalent about following up on the diagnosis made by her physician. Having taken care of both ailing parents largely by herself, Rita attributes her depression not primarily to grief, but to criticisms from older Black women in her community who accused her of not measuring up to their views of what a strong and dutiful daughter should do. In retrospect she notes, "when I didn't feel like my needs were being met, I got really depressed."

> I did *absolutely nothing for me*. And if you've ever taken care of someone who has cancer, you're up twenty-four hours a day. So really, I did *nothing* for me. . . . I felt so, I felt so smothered. And I didn't feel like, it wasn't as if I didn't *want* to take care of my parents, because I did. But, um, I, I also wanted help. And I *expected* that people would help me, and I didn't get it.

An audible resentment emerges in her recounting of the emergence of her depression, a period when she was left alone—by brothers and by community members—to manage her father's care at a stage when he could not eat, was weak, and could collapse at any moment. She describes herself as "angry" and "annoy[ed]" by "stupid, stupid neighbors . . . saying some really stupid shit, like, 'Oh well, Rita's here. I can stop doing now.' And they *constantly* said that."

Rita also acknowledges that she "never asked" for help, in part because she thought her needs were patently obvious—"How stupid could they be? You see me here working my *ass* off, you know, getting up every day. *Knowing* that my dad is having these spells where he just vomits, you know, or, you know, he lets it out another way." However, later in the interview she reveals another reason for not drawing attention to how "smothered" she felt:

> I think in the back of my mind, I didn't ask for help be-
> cause *they* [extended family members and the community]
> expected that I could do it. . . . You know, I don't like peo-
> ple to see me that way. Like I didn't want people to have a
> negative image or *bad* image of me.

Her desire to be favorably viewed by others outweighed her subjective sense of being overwhelmed. Reproached by an older woman
for not taking adequate care of her father, Rita recalls being painfully diminished by those words:

> So right away, like I could almost *feel* myself shrinking. So
> that was . . . *really* hard, and I still remember it today. There
> was always little comments like that, letting me know that
> I wasn't *living up* to these women's definitions of being
> strong. Of being, you know, being able to take care of
> things.

To avoid further upbraiding, Rita largely disconnected from her
sense of being beleaguered, and instead modified her behavior
and conscious focus so that she was "continually *trying to meet
everybody's expectations and demands.*" The emphases in her
words reflect the intensity of her embrace of this role and her subsequent efforts to appear strong. "And in fact, if you talk to people
here today, no one ever knew there was anything wrong with me.
Not anyone. I kept the façade up; I really did." The cost of doing so,
however, was her self-neglect, which "pushed me *further* into a
depression. So I was *only* able to exist for other people."

Although Rita is unique in openly discussing her clinical depression, her talk of its genesis and presence in her life overlaps with the extremes of strength behavior recounted by others. Such women speak of the risks of being too strong—a woman who, as Guerline describes, "forgets her *self*, you know. And she puts so much of *her* into her environment and her family and her entourage, *that's* when it [her strength] would become a weakness, because then the person has forgotten who *she* is. Where *her* needs are." Selflessness—a silencing and impending loss of the self—is the eventual end to a complete identification with being strong. Because it is "so easy for us to take on the superwoman role and put in overtime on everything," the woman who attempts to be a "twenty-four-hour woman" as Kiki was raised to be, and "do *everything* and anything . . . [will] die at the age of forty," notes Linda, a single woman in her early thirties. For these women, then, depression can be understood as exposing the fault line of strength—the convergence of undue demands and a compensatory strategy that forces them to live on two disconnected levels.

Conclusion

Overeating and depression emerge from the chafing of strength—with its restrictions and denials—on the bodies and minds of Black women. This friction occurs in part because Black women fight strength with strength. That is, they protest its injunctions by absorbing contradictions and only privately and indirectly acknowledging their discontent. Through what several call "internalization," Black women deny and discredit their knowledge of real and significant problems. As they expend considerable energy to keep their complex realities out of view, confined to an inner world, they embrace the lie of strength: that such actions are simply unremarkable or authenticating aspects of their lives. Significantly, however, internalization also reflects the women's divided consciousness: While their outward behavior is still largely aligned with the discourse, their minds are increasingly receptive to experiential reality. Consequently, they may state that overeating and depression are "white" problems, and yet acknowledge in hushed tones that such are not uncommon in their own lives or the lives of women they know and admire.

Although costly to a woman's well-being, overeating and depression are also muted protests. These problems of the body and mind importantly reveal the attempts of Black women to recognize states of duress, need, and exhaustion, which are impossible to express directly through talk of their strength. In angry or cautious tones, they acknowledge that their subjectivity is not limited to the stoicism, silence, and selflessness prescribed by strength. That is, despite performances to the contrary, these hurting Black women know they are much more than just strong.

Eating problems and depression do compromise wellness. However, they can also be turning points in women's lives. The private talk accompanying these states of distress speaks to a level of understanding about the impossibility of strength and the women's rights to a fuller existence. Significantly, the women describe these strivings as generated from within and not implanted from without. Over time, these women can develop a curiosity about their "deep down inside[s]" and an eventual commitment to such sources of insight. As Aisha observes from her own movement beyond strength, "Because we *all know*. When you're doing something that's out of *balance*, something that's going to *hurt you*, something that goes against the *grain, your spirit tells you*! . . . Even if you *deny* it to a certain extent, it *still* tells you." Not wholly conscious and often undermined by habitual self-silencing, the steady insistence of this experiential voice gestures toward what bell hooks (1993, 56) terms a "counter-system of valuation." Its existence reveals that strength's hold over Black women's subjectivity is formidable yet incomplete. Thus, when Black women take seriously these experiential voices, they become engaged in a careful reconsideration of the nature of "reality" and its relationship to the points of view they register as sincere and tied to their actual circumstances. It is such voices that allow Black women to work toward new traditions of expressiveness embedded in their lived experiences, rather than in the mandates of racialized gender.

5 / Coming to Voice

Transcending Strength

I think that Black women have got to begin to
think about what it means to *them* to be a woman.
And what did it mean to their mothers? What does
it mean in a larger culture? And then *try* to
determine the path. Even if it's a *lonely* path, a path
that leads to their *own* sort of self-fulfillment, no
matter what that means. . . . Again it's about
self-definition and *self*-confidence and *self*-esteem.
Those things need to be determined by us, and in
our individual situations.

—Sheila

I'm a strong Black woman, but not in the sense that
I'm willing to *carry* everything. I'm a strong Black
woman in that I make, I'm able to make *choices*,
and I now make choices on how *I* feel, and how it
affects me. And I think it takes *more* for a woman
to do that, than in other senses just to say, "Well, I'll
just be self-sacrificing and [let you] walk over me,"
you know. Because *I*, I'm at the point right now, I
don't mind getting the wrath from whomever, for
making *me* happy and giving me peace. . . . It
doesn't, to me, *pay* to be self-sacrificing. Because in
the *end*, you destroy your spirit. And you *lose*
yourself.

—Aisha

Voice is the expression of the "deep down inside" that Black women learn to create as they "pick up" strength. It reflects those points of view that locate Black women in their actual circumstances rather than in a timeless narration of struggle and caregiving. When Black women actively listen to what Kiki calls "these outlandish thoughts and feelings," they view these voices as instructive rather than weak or shameful. They also privilege experience over expectations, and refuse to allow strength to displace their humanity. They speak flexibly about what is really happening to them. And instead of fighting the expectation of strength with the silencing tactics of being strong, such women confront the discourse, not themselves, for its shortcomings. They recognize how it isolates Black women from the human family, how it covers over inequities, and how it thwarts their development and wellness. As they face their divided consciousness and question whose interests are served by strength, they firmly assert that they are inherently valuable—not because they suffer, survive, or care for others, but because they exist and are, undeniably, irreducibly human.

Voicing Paths Beyond Strength

A third of the interviewees did not primarily speak in or construct their realities through the discourse of strength. This group includes women who had never framed their lives within the discourse, and others who described developing past the expectation and strategy of "being strong." In common to all is a valuing of experiential reality over any external construction of their goodness. These women have voice.

While many of these voice-centered women use the word *strength* to discuss their lives, their talk lacks the discourse's steady association with self-neglect and ongoing self-harm. The synonyms they provide for their strength include *courage, maturity*, being *centered*, and achieving *balance*. Because they see through the mystique of strength and do not conflate its views with their own, they question its claims of their exceptionality. Illustrative of this ability is Monique's assertion: "I don't think that we're the only strong people in the world. . . . I am not that narrow-minded to think that God made us so much stronger than anybody else. . . . I think people have those expectations of us. I know they're not true." Able to distinguish their knowledge from the narrative of strength, they no longer exist as a "*double person*," living on two disconnected levels actively and laboriously maintained by silencing. Able to readily distinguish between an internal voice and an *internalized* voice (Gilligan [1982]1993), they experience a growth that Rita characterizes as "steadily defining what I want for *me*, as opposed to what other people want for me."

Voice-centered women see Black womanhood and strength as plural concepts, not reductively prescriptive ones. Unlike her foremothers whom she views as able to "take a lot more than any other race [or] sex," Linda characterizes herself and peers as "headstrong . . . [and] able to come into our own." They act "not because of circumstances, but just because that's what we want to do." They say "no" to requests that would overextend them, engage in physical exercise as a form of "me time," and generally develop a stance to the world that includes rather than excludes the self. In contrast to their strength-adhering counterparts, "headstrong" Black women seek physical and psychological "balance": between their needs and their concerns for others; between being capable and receiving help; and between respecting the work of foremothers and wanting to chart a new direction that includes selfknowledge, choice, and the ability to embrace multiple sides of their person.

At its core, strength redefined by these voice-centered women is predicated on self-care rather than self-neglect. They see themselves as fundamentally human, not "other" or exceptional. Continues Linda:

Every woman's going to cry once in a blue moon. That's our nature. That's being human. That's being female. That's being feminine. That's being sensitive as we are. But, pick your battles that you can fight, and fight those. And those battles that you fight, make sure you win them. And a strong Black woman does that. . . . The *strongest* woman knows how to say "no." And the strongest woman is . . . going to be able to support you, but she's not going to let herself *fail* because she's taking care of everybody else.

Openness, honesty, and mutuality are the qualities such women associate with their womanhood. As Savannah, a public relations consultant in her early twenties comments, the admission and revelation of hurt is, in fact, "the major part of being strong . . . being able to deal with *all* your characteristics and emotions. Being able to deal with the fact that you *will* need help, or you *are* vulnerable, or you *are* fearful, and that you *face* those characteristics or those challenges. And so you're not afraid to be yourself. . . . You're strong enough to say, 'I need help. I need assistance. Or, I need support.'" Strength is shifted from a prescription to a capacity they define. The view of strength promoted by these women is not, as the discourse maintains, a birthright to struggle for the exclusive benefit of others.

Such strength-critical women emphasize self-awareness and maturity. As a result, they avoid the extreme identification with strength, which results in, as thirty-three-year-old Amina describes, "someone who lets herself be driven all the time and either doesn't stop to think about what she wants or allows other things to overcome what she wants. . . . Someone who's unfulfilled to themselves." For these women, life is about development. The qualities they emphasize are, as Pilar, a government contractor and single mother of two describes, "growing . . . advancement . . . and not just settl[ing] for where I am," commitments that they also recognize "should be with *any* person, not just a Black woman." Because

they view change and growth over time as a human responsibility, they realize that "fulfilling my potential" is not met by the
traditional expectations placed on Black women to care for others
while neglecting themselves. Devoid of notions of ongoing sacrifice or extreme other-directedness, this voice-centered view of
strength allows for a scrutiny of why, to what ends, and for whom
a Black woman will put her abilities to use. Simple endurance,
such women conclude, is an insufficient definition of "living fully"
(hooks 1993, 137).

We're Vulnerable, and That Makes Us Human

Coming to voice about their existence as human (and not subhuman or superhuman) beings typically hinges on Black women
honoring their vulnerabilities. Whether in their own lives or in
their careful observation of the lives of women they love, they insist that Black women hurt and can be harmed. Doing so, they are
able to contrast the rhetoric of strength—what social critic Joan
Morgan hears as the assertion, "SBWs [Strong Black Women] don't
have needs"—with their own experiential realities—"I got plenty"
(1999, 86). Because they qualify and interrogate strength in personal terms, they demonstrate a keen awareness of its tolls, limitations, and distortions. Explains Nita, "Yes, we are strong, but we're
three-dimensional, or, as anyone else is.... [Strength is] not all
encompassing. It is not the *full* thing that defines [us]." She prefers
the term "brave" to "strong" in order to "recognize suffering. Like
if you see slave women, yes, they're strong, but they suffer. That's
brave. It encompasses strong and suffering in *one*." Attuned to
their own lives and health, they reject the excesses of self-denial
and self-silencing, which strength makes synonymous with their
lives as good women.

Critical of the dissociations occasioned by strength, such
women describe themselves as having complementary rather than

mutually exclusive emotional states and needs. At a basic level, strength-critical women assert that no narrative of exceptionality or virtue should thwart a person's ability to recognize that, as Micheline, a guidance counselor, articulates, "we're still underneath that flesh and blood. So we're still vulnerable." They realize the trap of strength, that "to keep saying you are strong all the time strips you of the ability to say, 'I'm vulnerable and I'm hurting.' And that can throw you into a chasm, where you're facing, um . . . [sigh] crises." To develop self-protective sensibilities about their needs and contexts, they, like married educator Anika, realize a powerful difference between the perception of Black women "never hav[ing] problems" and a fraudulent *constructed* reality in which "we're not *allowed* to" reveal distress. It is their attention to lived experiences and voice that allows them to move from precipices of self-loss including ill health, damaging relationships, or a sense of nonexistence.

In the wake of the clinical depression she experienced after losing both parents and "having brothers and seeing family members really just take advantage of me," Rita conveys a clarity of vision about her humanity and value. Taking her anger and feelings of violation seriously allowed to her conclude, "Enough is enough. I've got to put myself *first* because no on else is and no one else cares." This shift in vantage point also required that she realize her internalization of strength's prescriptions, "that I was really *locked* into a pattern of taking care of everyone else but myself," because of her acceptance of the dictum that "a strong woman should care for *everyone* and leaves herself out."

Despite the apparent alignment of much of her psyche and behavior with strength, Rita speaks of the transformation from self-exclusion to self-inclusion as an organic process. In a quietly reflective voice she states, "Even when I was younger . . . I've always had this part of me that's said, 'You know, some of this is just not right'. . . . So part of me has always been somewhat defiant, acceptably defiant, about what I want for myself." It is this voice that had long supported counter-practices to her strength, which included regular athletic activity and meditation. While not preventing her from becoming highly identified with the deeply held cultural value of strength, these traditions of contemplation did allow her eventual detachment from strength, enabling her to "witness these things that are going on" without becoming a "*character* in these plays." Thus, when she was brought to an emotional and relational nadir from her performance of strength, these practices of self-care offered a sustaining alternative.

Increasingly committed to recognizing the self that was submerged by strength, Rita expresses a remarkable sense of freedom and joy about her current existence. With a contagious effervescence she says, "What really makes me ... [a] human being [giggle] ... is a balance of both weakness and strength. Because weakness and strength affects every aspect of humanity. You know, it touches on you being vulnerable. ... So there's really not any aspect of me I can't talk about when I think of myself as being both weak and strong."

From years of "picking up" strength and later submerging her discontent through compulsive overeating, Traci has come to a similar conviction about her humanity. She now recognizes that although "[strength's] the way you're being taught," health and wellness remain elusive until "you ... grow out of it. Or eventually, as a grown woman, find something that works for you." Traci's loss of sixty pounds and avoidance of diabetes required that she see and squarely question the depleting service of strength:

> Years ago, I wanted to make sure *everybody* was happy. There's no way, *in the world*, you can ever make sure everybody is happy. And you try to play that superwoman role, where you *try* your best. ... And that's just not how life goes [chuckle]. I mean, sincerely, it's *not* how life goes, and I found that out.

She credits a daily walking routine not simply with her weight loss but with liberating a voice of her own. Particularly striking is how she describes "being free, out in the air, the wind blowing," the time alone allowing for a direct expression of her needs:

> And you *think*, and when you walk and think, then you try to figure out, "Well, what's best for me right now? What type of woman do I want to be *right now*?" And then you start putting things into perspective, because then I *divorced*.... Yes, I started walking, and I said, "This isn't. I'm *not* happy. And if I'm not happy, I don't have to portray this role anymore that for him I'm going to be happy."... You have to make a decision to go out and help yourself, and then you're no longer thinking for just your daughter. You're thinking for *you*, as an African American woman. Because once you're dead and gone, nobody's going to know *what* happened, why you kept it inside.

Through walking, Traci was able to focus on her subjective appraisal of life, and not simply on her dependents and their needs and expectations of her. Being able to step behind these demands, she uncovered and regained a "voice" and an "identity" that she then used to question and distance herself from the role of strength: "I had time to think, and then, you know, deal with who I am. Who, basically, I am.... I took control over my life, then.... I started thinking, and I started becoming *bold* [chuckle], I started making decisions, and I'm talking *later*.... In my late thirties." Walking was an outlet that amplified rather than muted Traci's voice. Wisdom and maturity now supplant Traci's former commitment to strength.

A similar turn toward self-defined womanhood is expressed by Marie as "one of the things that I had to learn ... through my experience." As a young girl in Haiti, she was raised with two "contrast[ing]" models of womanhood: her mother, who "never took responsibility for her own life," and a paternal aunt who, as a teenager, raised nine younger siblings and later became a highly regarded "*pillar*" of her rural community. Like many Black women, Marie was drawn to the caring and independence of her aunt as the more positive example of womanhood. However, as an adult in her thirties, she eventually recognized disturbing parallels between how both she and her aunt were exploited, particularly in intimate relationships, for being "*too* good."

> If there is *one* woman on this *planet Earth* who deserves to have a man who would worship the soil that she walks on, she was my auntie. Because she was a *godly* woman, a good woman, a respectful woman, an educated [woman]. . . . But her husband did not appreciate that. Everything about my auntie was intimidating to him, and then he treated her like dirt. . . . The man failed to realize that [this] woman was the right-hand person who could help him to succeed.

While not detailing her own encounters with "parasitic personalities," Marie does discuss a momentous shift away from what she calls her "mother syndrome."

> Because the more you give, the more people want to take. . . . So, it was liberating for me when I realized that I was nobody's savior. Jesus has already done that so that I don't need to do it. And I, I got a revelation that, "Hey, if I die tomorrow, nobody's going to put themselves in the grave with me. I'm going alone." That means everyone has a way of surviving without me. So, don't hold on to me like if I was your very lifeline.

Marie resists the martyrdom of strength by no longer accepting the pressure to be everyone's rescuer. Stepping away from the over-responsibility she had associated with dutiful goodness, she now maintains that "love, and friendship, and affection, they go both ways. So, don't, don't be accustomed to *getting* from me. You know, ask me what you can do for me.... If you ... have to be around me because I can do something for you, then you have *no genuine* love and affection for me." Like other strength-critical, voice-centered women, Marie refuses strength's goal of dictating an existence commensurate with situations of oppression and the ideological and personal needs of others.

For most Black women, mothers and mother-figures are the persons from whom they learned to "pick up" this racialized construction of gender. However, appreciating their mothers beyond the script of strength is key to finding answers to their own questions about possibilities beyond self-sacrifice and self-harm. As a result, coming to voice for many Black women entails seeing their mothers as human beings and not simply as icons to emulate. They examine what their mothers accomplished but also what such women *lost* by adhering to a strength-defined notion of goodness. Like Macy, they can, for example, sympathetically understand a mother as a woman who self-protectively hides her emotional hurt in excess weight, who "was looking for love in the wrong places, and ... found it in *men*, and then when *men* let her down, she found it in *food*." Such careful observations allow them to break away from expectations that threaten not only their mothers' humanity, but their own.

As seen in Marie's description of her aunt, too often the self-sacrifice of strong women is enlisted to support the patriarchal aspirations of male partners. Appeals to Black women's strength in marriages encourage what Sheila names as men's problematic willingness to "*use* our bodies and our dreams and our minds and our spirits to *fund* or *finance* their own projects ... or to *make their manhood*, or to increase their masculine stock." Sheila causally relates her mother's periodic breakdowns to the inequities in her parents' marriage. As a "*strong superwoman*," her mother has had myriad paid and unpaid "jobs ... [that] go on and on and on and on" in support of the family. Although she credits her mother for being "our angel on earth" and a nurturing "tree . . . who stood in the water . . . in the rain for me and made a shelter for me," she also questions what strength should mean to her as she lives her own life. Examining the lack of reciprocity experienced by her mother in the marriage, she sees that "trying to be a superwoman is *not* or should not really be the goal of a woman's life. . . . There's a price." For all of her giving, her mother rarely received the recognition she deserved in return: "You know, the kind of love that she wants, the kind of relationship that she wants. The kind of *thanks* and appreciation that she wants."

Currently unmarried, Sheila and her sisters envision a "sort of a higher standard of what a man needs to be." They seek partnerships in which a man "can't be trying to hold for dear life to, you know, this role that makes him feel like he's this *man* when the way that a man is defined can be *many* different things, depending on responsibilities. Depending on situation and circumstance." Understanding their mothers in complex terms—as strong and vulnerable, courageous and afraid, loving and exhausted—these daughters realize that claims of strength are not a proxy for any woman's humanity.

Instructively, women who are able to describe mothers as multifaceted feeling persons resist the categorization of these women—or any Black woman—as "strong" and not fully human. Kim, a twenty-eight-year-old higher education administrator, credits her mother for the ability to manage a Black woman supervisor's pressure to become a similar "never-let-them-see-you-sweat kind of woman." Recalling how she was subjected to an hour-long verbal thrashing for crying in the office, she staunchly rejects her boss's view of her emotional expressiveness as problematic.

You would have thought I stole a million dollars. . . . She *dragged* me into my office and she slammed the door, and she said, "You will *not cry* in front of anyone. You are a

strong Black woman!" . . . And this went on for an hour. . . . .
And she was *very* disappointed in me, and . . . she didn't
ever want to see me do that again. And I thought, "I am a
human being. And I am overwhelmed. . . . [Yet] instead of
your worrying about my well-being and how I'm doing,
you're berating me because I let you down as a Black
woman!?"

While taken aback by such severe chastisement, Kim countered
her boss's charge of strength—at least psychologically—by drawing on her mother's words regarding the validity of her emotions.
From childhood, she had heard that "it's not right to stuff emotions or act like someone that you're not, because you're a human
being. You have feelings." Accustomed to defining her humanity
outside of strength, she is not easily persuaded by others' attempts
to put her in a particular place of subordination. As a result, when
hearing the term "strong Black woman," she quickly and simply
remarks, "I don't think it really *means* anything."

Micheline also grounds her resistance to strength in the emotional openness evidenced by her mother. From age ten she recalls
understanding the pressures bearing down on her mother, a divor-
cee left with minimal support from her ex-husband. A transformative experience for her was seeing the tears most other women were
actively discouraged from witnessing by their similarly stressed
mothers.

I mean, I saw my mom cry. I saw her have meltdowns
where she would say, "I just. This is just too much. I can't,"
you know, and so, but I still, I didn't see her as *weak* though.
I saw her as being overwhelmed, having a lot on her plate.
But, she picked . . . herself up and said, "Okay. I've had my
moment, and I just have to keep going." So yeah, I think
when you talk about strength, I think it says that you're
vulnerable as well.

Micheline describes this revelation as "a tender moment," which enabled her to recognize that "my mom is human" but not "think any less of her. In fact, after having seen her crying and just knowing all the stuff that she was going through, I felt she was a very strong person." Her mother had not simply an uninflected strength but courage to press on while acknowledging her fears. A nuanced notion of her mother's capacities and sacrifices informs Micheline's appreciation of Black women as human beings.

We're Human Beings . . . *First*

Recognizing vulnerability is one facet of Black women resisting their exceptionality. A second process entails finding ways to uphold their humanity despite the discourse's attempts to accommodate them to a lesser status. Assertions of their humanity create an effective "counter-system of valuation" (hooks 1993, 56) that attenuates strength's dominance in their lives and affirms their social place as actors with value equal to those around them.

For some women, it is a newfound spirituality that reinforces the experiential voice within that strength so adamantly rejects. This spirituality very intentionally recognizes their humanity, and legitimizes their aspirations beyond strength. As Marie expresses, it was during her thirties that she sought and achieved a "balance" and reached "a place where . . . I form my own opinion, and I make my own decisions. And right now my standard is the following. . . . As long as I can justify my decision before God and my conscience is clear, I don't care what anybody else says. Because people will always have their own opinion, regardless."

Aisha credits a comparable valuation of herself to a plaque received from an elderly woman in her church. Its message—"God's gift to you is your life. And what you make out of your life is your gift to God"—validates her desire for mutuality and recognition in her interactions with others. Very significantly, its words amplified the stirrings of her subjectivity at a critical moment in her life.

> And, I just got to a point where when you look at it, you make so many sacrifices for *people*, but people continue to live the way they want to live. . . . I looked at my *age*, and I looked at where I had *been* and the life I was living, and I was like, "I don't want to be sitting down somewhere when I'm old and saying, 'I *could* have did this. I *should* have did this.' But I *didn't* because of this person or that person, and they *did* what they wanted to do." . . . You know, some people, granted, it's *fine* for them to take care of other people. But I'm *more* than that. And I *want* more than that. And sometimes, even though I have *major* inner conflict, because *believe me*, I have inner conflict. But I just put it to the side, and I'm like [to God], "You know my heart. You know what I want. And you know what I need and what I'm trying to do." And I just bypass it and keep going.

With this philosophy encountered and adopted well into her thirties, Aisha no longer measures her worth and goodness by the extent to which she, as a Black woman, is *"completely self-sacrificing."* Rather than answer to the discourse of strength, Aisha and others describe having responsive relationships with a spiritual being who is "someone who *listens* as well as directs and dictates, who . . . is experienced as 'in me'" (Rule Goldberger 1996, 348). Such emphasis on reciprocation and voice also manifests in Aisha's refusal to continue accepting infidelity among men, despite observing this resignation in the behavior of her mother and other strong women of her community.

Pamela speaks of coming to voice as a process of redefining herself as "divinely made." Generalizing from her personal experience, she states that to achieve "maturity," a Black woman has to "grow beyond her Blackness" and reconsider much of what she has long held as true and significant in her life.

> That's the bottom line. It's not that she's Black that *makes* her who she is; it's actually inside her *spirit*, that, you know, gives her who she really is.... If she turns to her spiritual, you know, turns to God first, understanding *why* she's called to do such things, I think it'll help her to realize that everything that people are depending on you to do... *God* is not necessarily asking you to do those things.... Some things you have to say "no" to; some things you have to say "yes" to. So I think it's a matter of giving her balance, so she'll know what to take on, and what not to.

Being "connected to that inner, you know, strength from God" is a corrective to "getting to the point where you're finally burned out. And you realize, you know, 'There's got to be more to this life than what I'm doing.'" Speaking in the third person but autobiographically, Pamela describes recovering from an extensive loss of self: "Because basically, what she does is start to, when she's trying to handle all these things, she begins to deteriorate herself, almost like *she's* disappearing." Reaching a point when she was able to say, "No more. I'm burned out. I won't do it," allowed her to begin "letting go and then the balance can begin to come in." Pamela's evocative description of strength-induced distress vividly recalls Kiki's profound conclusion that "it's not possible to do all, and be successful at all, and try to, without hurting yourself." These women verify the costs of strength in terms both stark and familiar to many Black women.

Such voice-centered spirituality typically draws on a language of inherent value and mutuality significantly stripped of references to race or gender. While not discounting the real effects of social inequities in the world, Rita cautions against taking these social constructions as fixed accounts for how Black women need to engage themselves and others.

> Being able to define *who* you are is something that all human beings should do. . . . It's *really* dangerous for us to say we have nothing in common with other human beings. I mean, you really have to take it to that level, because that's what we are *first*. . . . We're human beings who are Black, who are white, who are, you know, Puerto Rican. . . . And, as I said, I think that a lot of people, Black, white, whatever, use "we have nothing in common" as a catalyst or motivator, to keep differences, to keep us apart, and to add fuel to an existing fire.

Her insistence that "We're human beings . . . *first*" directly assails the singularity attached to being Black and female in society, and validates a wariness about such claims of exclusivity and incommensurability.

Conclusion

Acknowledging their vulnerabilities and insisting on their humanity, strength-critical women assert that they are "mules" no more. Able to hold experiential knowledge against the prescriptions and lies of strength, they develop the clarity to distinguish what "needs to be done . . for [one's] life" from the discourse-driven insistence that "I have to do everything." Differentiating voice from discourse, they resist "being what others expect or what you don't want to be." This is a critical shift that many associate with moving toward balance, mutuality, wellness, and joy in their lives.

Appreciating voice, these strength-critical women realize that a diversity exists within and among "Black women." They do not trivialize their humanity in the name of virtues experienced as cloying, false, and impossible to maintain without hurting the self. They understand that "emotional well-being [is] just as important as the collective struggle to end racism and sexism—that indeed these two experiences are linked" (hooks 1993, 139). As they recognize their vulnerability and insist on their shared humanity with others, Black women articulate that they—their minds, bodies, emotional and physical health, and dreams—matter. Consequently, rather than strength, wellness and self-care become cornerstones of their existence. And as they discuss their lives and aspirations, their accounts markedly lack the silence, resignation, and distress so prominent among other women interviewed. Coming to voice, they resist a particularly pernicious construction of racialized gender.

As Black women recognize and listen to this empirical voice, often a daughter's voice,[1] the discourse loses its hold over them as the moral standard for evaluating their goodness. They start to question their exceptionality—"I shouldn't have to make it through everything . . . [and] fight the battle that no one else has to fight." They resist constructions of their singularity for erecting a deceitful pedestal that renders them into spectacles to be admired or harshly critiqued, but always from a distance. As they question such fixed contrasts between themselves and all other race–gender groups, they become able to speak of both fulfillment and vulnerability in their lives. Furthermore, they make their humanity visible to themselves, and to others willing to see and hear beyond strength. By embracing their complete subjectivity, they also minimize the designations of minority race and gender as lesser human forms. Taking the fact of their voice seriously, they implicitly appreciate Kesho Scott's (1991, 226) caution that "In our silences, we are tragically doomed to create 'habits of survival,' always to adapt ourselves to the temporal and changing guises of ongoing racial, sexual, and class oppression."

Epilogue: Mules No More, Just "Levelly Human"

A Societal Challenge

We reject pedestals, queenhood, and walking ten paces behind. To be recognized as human, levelly human, is enough.

— The Combahee River Collective Statement

Black women really have a story to tell. If we *ever bonded*, it would be . . . an *awesome moment*. And it would be a lot of tears shed, but it would be an awesome moment. We have, we *share so much*, but we can't share it with each other. We share the same lives. We go through many of the *same struggles*. The *same depressions*. . . . If we started to *acknowledge our pain* as a society of people, [as] Black women, *my God!* That pain would extend *way back*, to when massa was raping the women. Because that's where it started. And we would have to take on *all that*, and I think it's so much easier for us to just [say], "Hey, you're okay. You're fine. Don't even worry about that. Oh, that's just a small cut; go put something on that and go."

—Jennifer

Oppressed groups have long understood that systems of domination trade not only in material disparities but in lies. Whether named as myths, mystiques, sincere fictions, or controlling images, these falsehoods distort what is known, felt, desired, and accomplished in order to justify inequality. Taken in as truths, such deceptions have the power to profoundly compromise our abilities to achieve justice in our lives.

The opening epigraphs are salvos to transcend racialized gender. The first by the Combahee River Collective (1982, 16) is a charge to society as a whole. Drafted in the 1970s, the simple assertion that Black women are "levelly human" strikes at the heart of the matrix of domination, its hierarchies of social worth, and its foundational binary oppositions. If the group long treated as "de mule uh de world" (Neale Hurston 1937, 14) is human, then accepted asymmetries of value become highly problematic. Specifically, racialized gender and its controlling imagery are revealed to be wholly antithetical to our nation's principles, which affirm that no group has natural claims of superiority or ownership over others; that all individuals are self-determining; and that it is an inalienable right for citizens to live freely and fully.

However, as Kim Chernin ([1982]1994, 2) reminds us, ours is "a culture that is seriously divided within itself, splitting itself off from nature, dividing the mind from the body, dividing thought from feeling, dividing one race against another, dividing the supposed nature of woman from the supposed nature of man." Racialized gender is evident in our country's policies of subordination, segregation, and separation; our social practices effecting physical and emotional distances between groups; and our states of psychic dissociation. We are thus all implicated: Our humanity is crippled and our possibilities limited when we tell and retell—as if they were true, as if they were necessary—stories of racialized gender.

The second epigraph directs a challenge from a Black woman to Black women. It is voiced by Jennifer, a woman who identifies with strength not because she is taken in by the lie, but because she lacks the community in which to explore alternatives. Her words are an impassioned appeal to Black women to no longer allow the distortions and silences of strength to compromise their individual humanity and their relationships with each other. As she expresses, "*acknowledg[ing] our pain*" has the potential to allow Black women to see and proactively engage with the reality that "we *share so much*... the same lives.... The *same struggles. The same depressions.*" Hers is a desperate plea for bonds of sisterhood that staunchly and consciously refuse to propagate the lies of strength. However, as she very reluctantly concedes, the path of least resistance for too many Black women is that of continued silences, to say to each other, in spite of all evidence to the contrary, "'Hey, you're okay. You're fine.'"

Taken together, both quotes call for race–gender groups to speak up and back to strength as a form of "everyday activism" (Phillips 2006, xxx). Racialized gender as a form of domination exists because it is "done" (West and Zimmerman 1987)—that is, brought into existence—by all of us, through our unexamined habits of thought and behavior. When we use "strength" as an excuse to extort thankless, degrading work from Black women, in their homes or in their workplaces; when we appeal to this narrative of invulnerability to justify predatory social policies that blame victims of poverty, abuse, and neglect for not being "strong enough" to transcend these socially created barriers to wellness and full citizenship; when we excuse our misbehavior in intimate or public settings by preemptively claiming that, as Black women, they can "take it"; when we teach our daughters that strength is a badge they must earn through extremes of suffering and reservoirs of silence; when we see mental and physical wellness as carrying a "'Whites Only' sign" (Head 2004, 22)—we are each "doing" strength and contributing mightily to the structure and seeming permanence of racialized gender. Such uses of the lie of strength to mask the dissonance between ideals and social reality thus demonstrate our abiding allegiance to a world that patriarchy and slavery have created in flagrant disregard of the humanistic principles of democracy.

It is in these common, daily routines that the undoing (Deutsch 2007) of racialized gender needs to occur. Explains Layli Phillips (2006, xl):

> While institutions can be problematic, what is more problematic are the thought processes, emotional structures, attitudes, and social practices that make such institutions, and indeed the relations of oppression and domination wherever they manifest, possible in the first place.... [I]n the absence of changed minds and changed practices, dismantled social institutions will only re-form in newly oppressive ways.

Thus, when coworkers and employers no longer mete out workloads and benefits based on making the distinction between Black "women" and white "ladies"; when family members and friends listen to and take seriously a Black girl's hurts and respect these vulnerabilities as a precious part of her humanity and her right to live with integrity; when partners extend themselves toward Black women through ongoing commitments of care, recognition, and trust (hooks 2000a, 5); when Black women tend to their bodies and minds as much as they guard those of others in their care, we take active steps away from a plantation society structured on racialized gender, and move toward practicing democracy as our real legacy.

The question posed to all of us is whether we will marshal the courage to set ourselves and each other free from the ruses of racialized gender, to give up the lies of strength, for the simple justice of seeing Black women—and all people—as "levelly human."

Acknowledgments

I t takes a village to raise a child, and a community to nurture an idea into maturity. While the thoughts and arguments of this book are my own, they developed over many years within several networks of intellectual and moral support.

I wish to express a debt of gratitude to the following:

- Carol Gilligan, whose seminal work on voice has provided much inspiration and direction to my own quest to portray Black women as complex social beings with psychological depth. At critical times, she offered the necessary resonance for my emerging ideas.
- Becky Thompson, an intellectual maverick whose work on the embodiment struggles of women of color and precious friendship have been most sustaining.
- Janie V. Ward, a longtime mentor who has guided my professional growth with a unique balance of shrewd insight, compassion, and humor.

- Thomas S. Dickinson, the incarnation of Erik Erikson's concept of "generativity," a dear friend, and a patient advisor through a writing process new to me and so familiar to him.
- Faculty development funds at DePauw University, and specifically the generosity of Dr. William Asher and the Janet Prindle Institute for Ethics, which have provided me with the time and support to focus my energies at various stages of research and writing.
- Lesa Carter, Janine Ekulona, Ronda Henry, Mechthild Kiegelmann, Guitele Nicoleau, and Dhelia Williamson, for their ongoing sisterhood and willingness to listen patiently to many nascent ideas and fragile connections.
- Jo Holt, for her reassurance that darkness often precedes clarifying light.
- Ted Jelen, who extended friendship and sage counsel when these were least expected but most needed.
- Mick Gusinde-Duffy, my editor at Temple University Press, who from our first e-mails saw directly into the soul of this project and provided the gentle encouragement to release it in words.
- My parents Gladys and Fritz Beauboeuf, as well as my siblings Régine and Marc, my husband Pascal Lafontant, and our children Dominique and Milo, who have accompanied me on this journey and witnessed the joyful burden I've carried for the last eight years.
- The women I've met over the life of this project, who opened my eyes and my heart to their eloquence and resilience as fully human beings. I have tried to be a dutiful student of their careful instruction regarding how much more than "just strong" Black women really are.

Earlier versions of arguments found in this text appeared in the following:

Beauboeuf-Lafontant, Tamara. "Listening past the lies that make us sick: A voice-centered analysis of strength and depression in Black women." *Qualitative Sociology* 31, no. 4 (2008): 391–406.

Beauboeuf-Lafontant, Tamara. "'You have to show strength': An exploration of gender, race, and depression," *Gender & Society* 21, no. 1 (2007): 28–51.

Beauboeuf-Lafontant, Tamara. "Keeping up appearances, getting fed up: The embodiment of strength among African American women," *Meridians* 5, no. 2 (2005): 104–123.

Beauboeuf-Lafontant, Tamara. "Strong and large Black women? Exploring relationships between deviant womanhood and weight," *Gender & Society* 17, no. 1 (2003): 111–121.

Appendix: Table of Participants

	Pseudonym	Age	Occupation,* parental status, marital status
1.	Aisha	36	Bank employee/student, single
2.	Aleah	27	Administrative assistant, single, mother
3.	Alexis	23	Global sourcing manager, mother, single
4.	Allene	50	Administrative assistant, mother, married
5.	Amina	33	International development manager, mother, single
6.	Angie	24	Student, single
7.	Anika	34	Educator, mother, married
8.	Anouk	49	Educator, mother, married
9.	Audrey	52	Educator, mother, single
10.	Brenda	50	Higher education administrator, single
11.	Celia	40	Health educator, single
12.	Crystal	36	Student, mother, single
13.	Dana	30	Librarian, mother, married
14.	Deidre	25	Higher education administrator, single
15.	Denise	25	Media officer, mother, married
16.	Guerline	39	After school director, married
17.	Gwendolyn	24	Student
18.	Jayne	32	International development manager, mother, married
19.	Jennifer	29	Bank employee/student, mother, divorced
20.	Joy	32	Higher education administrator, mother, single
21.	Karyn	25	Advertising assistant, single
22.	Kiki	24	Medical technician, mother, single
23.	Kim	28	Higher education administrator, married
24.	Kira	22	Student, single

(continued)

	Pseudonym	Age	Occupation,* parental status, marital status
25.	Layla	22	Student, single
26.	Linda	31	Corporate cash manager, single
27.	Lynda	27	Educator, married
28.	Macy	21	Student, single
29.	Madeleine	41	Database analyst, single
30.	Marie	39	Educator, divorced
31.	Martha	66	Retired health professional, mother, married
32.	Marva	47	Machine operator, mother, married
33.	Micheline	34	Educator, mother, married
34.	Michelle	21	Teacher's aide/student, single
35.	Milly	32	Graphic artist, single
36.	Monique	39	Program manager, mother, married
37.	Morgan	45	Community organizer, mother, married
38.	Nita	36	Higher education administrator, married
39.	Pamela	37	Stylist, mother, married
40.	Patrice	67	Retired upholsterer, mother, divorced
41.	Pilar	31	Government contractor, mother, single
42.	Portia	20	Student, single
43.	Reena	25	Student
44.	Rita	35	Graduate student, single
45.	Rosha	19	Student, single
46.	Savannah	23	Public relations consultant, single
47.	Sharon	45	Educator, single
48.	Shay	55	Information sciences coordinator, mother, married
49.	Sheila	35	College educator, single
50.	Sondra	46	Student, mother, married
51.	Sophie	62	Homemaker, mother, married
52.	Soraya	45	Student, mother
53.	Tamika	40	Public health officer, single
54.	Tanya	22	Student, single
55.	Tasha	33	Police officer/student, mother, married
56.	Traci	43	Student, mother, divorced
57.	Yasmin	32	Educator, single
58.	Yvonne	57	Mother, divorced

* In earlier phases of the study, occupation was not requested of participants.

Notes

Introduction

1. Historian Nell Irvin Painter (1996) provides a critical examination of both the myth of Sojourner Truth's resilience and the available facts of her life. Arguing that the 1851 "Ar'n't I a woman?" speech attributed to Truth was fabricated by Francis Dana Gage twelve years after the fact, Irvin Painter maintains that this gripping soliloquy was based on the racist construction of Truth as a figure who existed outside of and in spite of slavery and sexism. Irvin Painter highlights the difficulty both academic and lay contemporary audiences experience when presented with a more complex, less unidimensional depiction of Truth than the "strong Black woman" image allows. As Irvin Painter reluctantly concludes, "The symbol of Sojourner Truth is stronger and more essential in our culture than the complicated historic person. . . . I can explain to you the making of the symbol of Sojourner Truth, the electrifying black presence in a white crowd. But I cannot talk you out of the convictions you need to get through life. The symbol we require in our public life still triumphs over scholarship" (287).

2. All names for interviewed women are pseudonyms.

3. Throughout the quoted interview material, text emphasized in the original is set in italics.

4. The concept of voice powerfully emerged in the social sciences with Carol Gilligan's 1982 publication of *In a Different Voice: Psychological Theory*

and Women's Development. This text opened the door to listening carefully to interview data to distinguish different reference points for meaning-making that could be aligned with, as well as resistant to, dominant forms of femininity.

5. Most published uses of the Listening Guide have critically examined aspects of hegemonic gender socialization, such as adolescent female sexuality (Tolman 2002); anger among girls (Brown 1998) and women (Crowley Jack 1999b); girls' relationships with each other (Brown 2005) and adult women (McLean Taylor, Gilligan, and Sullivan 1996); boys' understanding of their same-sex friendships (Chu 2005); and women's experiences of depression (Crowley Jack 1991). Although developed and primarily utilized to analyze the psychosocial realities of white, middle-class women's experiences of gender subordination, there is little in the Guide to preclude its use to empirically investigate the voices of other groups as well as the specific gender discourses through which they are perceived. Tensions between discourses and voices, between normalized representations and subjectivity, are central features of contemporary configurations of power in a race-, class-, and gender-stratified society. My own use of the Guide begins with the premise that the shared meanings and ideological interests of discourses largely structure the kinds of narratives about self and others told. Thus, instead of assuming hegemonic femininity to be present in interview data, I looked for evidence of a particular construction of femininity—in this case, strong Black womanhood—and evaluated the ways in which it affects the thought and behavior of the women I interviewed.

6. The research was advertised as a study of perceptions of womanhood and beauty. *Behind the Mask* focuses on the data relating to womanhood, which developed into a rich focus requiring sustained attention.

7. The term "Black" has been contentious, and in this book I use it to refer generally to women of African descent. I find that across ethnic, cultural, socioeconomic, and age contexts, the term and experiences of being a "strong Black woman" are widely intelligible.

8. As I explore further in this book, by naturalizing particular qualities—such as extremes of devotion, and physical and emotional endurance—the invocation of strength shores up boundaries between "strong" Black women and their "weak" white counterparts. This reflects, in part, the rootedness of the discourse of strength in a much larger system of oppression based on the creation and opposition of several race–gender groups.

9. Wallace, Michele ([1978]1990).

Chapter 1

1. Even within the political projects of Black men and white women, Black women's own standpoints on social reality have historically been ignored, distorted, or actively minimized. A significant portion of this erasure has been managed by claims of Black women's exceptional strength (Wallace 1990, 227). As a result, the reluctance and sometimes outright refusal of white women and Black men to adopt an intersectional approach to their subordination as well as to oppression generally has typically left Black women with the ironic experience of being "completely silenced" yet represented in these groups as though they were "powerful, articulate, and invulnerable" (Hill Collins 2005, 227)—as if their social disadvantages coalesced to form a peculiar advantage. As a result, Black women gain token acceptance in these movements to the extent that they suppress the contradictions inherent in examining only race or gender rather than points of their intersection in understanding and moving against oppression (hooks 2000b; Scott 1991).

2. The continued efficacy of such constructs is evident in their contemporary formulations. Images of "bad" or "undesirable" welfare queens and homicidal gangsters trade on such historically "sedimented" (Hill Collins 2005, 120) associations of an essential hypersexuality and proclivity to violence among Black women and men, particularly those from the poor and working classes. As a result, such groups are subject to punitive policies designed to contain their reproduction, physical movement, and social mobility for the benefit and safety of white "civil" society (Arnett Ferguson 2001; Richie 1995; Roberts 1997).

3. One can productively view the discourse of strength as dictating particular "feeling rules," which Black women strive to follow by engaging in performances or what Arlie Russell Hochschild (1979) refers to as "emotion management." As I explore in later chapters, such emotion work is costly to Black women and can become embodied in the distresses of overeating and depression. However, my focus on voice also reveals that despite the "deep acting" of emotion work, individuals can critique and resist such feeling rules as well as the "patterns of social membership" (Russell Hochschild 1979, 566) upheld by these emotional guidelines.

4. Trudier Harris (1995) characterizes strength as a "disease," which encourages Black women to take a domineering approach to family members. Focused on literary representations of such mothers, her work suggests the need for further empirical examinations of the relational costs of strength.

5. Elaine Bell Kaplan's (1997) ethnography of low-income Black teenage mothers lends support to Wallace's earlier observations and contentions. As

they traverse adolescence, Bell Kaplan contends that such girls are too often "deprived of every resource needed for any human being to function well in our society: education, jobs, food, medical care, a secure place to live, love and respect, the ability to securely connect with others" (10). In contrast to "the insidious and insistent stereotyping of them as promiscuous and aberrant teenage girls," Bell Kaplan finds that these adolescents lack fundamental knowledge about their bodies, exert virtually no agency as sexual subjects, and uncritically accept relationships with men on sexist terms (10). As a result, such girls are not the notorious beings of sexist and racist imagery, but incredibly vulnerable, often naïve, misled, and underloved children largely at the mercy of adult forces and male-centered institutions.

Chapter 2

1. The internalization and individualization of eating problems and depression discredit women's anger. They also demonstrate the reining in of women's thoughts and emotions to adhere to cultural constructions of a compliant femininity. Anger is a particularly threatening emotion because its expression "is intimately tied to self-respect, to the capacity to direct one's life. For this reason, women's anger is often considered . . . an act of insubordination" (Crowley Jack 2003, 66). More common among women than expressions of anger, therefore, are actions that reflect women's "implicit loyalty to the conventional world" (Chernin [1982]1994, 108; see also, Ussher 2004). Thus a temporary break from the tyranny of discourses predicated on the active devaluation of subjective knowing is repaired by a woman's socialization in the feminine policing tactics of denial, internalization, and self-blame.

2. By leading women to absorb and psychologize, rather than externalize and politicize their discontent, the controlling image of white, ultrafeminine (Morton 1991) beauty enlists such women and their bodies in the doing rather than "undoing" of a particular formulation of gender (Deutsch 2007). Beauty reveals itself to be a "regim[e] of knowledge through which women come to recognize themselves as 'woman,' judging themselves as good or bad, mad or sane in relation to their adherence to representations of the ideal" (Ussher 2004, 256). Providing a self-scrutinizing and self-blaming focus and assigning a barrage of body work for women rightfully disgruntled with their lives compared to what they desire or can imagine, "the beauty myth is not about women [or beauty] at all. It is about men's institutions and [the protection of their] institutional power" (Wolf 1991, 13). Idealizing a pared-down version of women's bodies, such imagery represents good women not only as thin and young, but as powerless on their own, incapable of holding

positions of social influence, and hampered by bodies that are fundamentally flawed and require constant improvement.

3. About two-thirds of adult Black women, age eighteen and older, are considered overweight, as compared to 60% of Latino populations, 47% of white women, and 25% of Asian/Pacific Islander women (Leigh and Huff, 2006, 74). With regard to obesity, defined as having a Body Mass Index of 30 or above, the pattern remains, with 35% of Black women, 26% of Latino women, 20% of white women, and 6.2% of Asian/Pacific Islander women meeting the diagnostic criteria (Leigh and Huff 2006, 73). The tendency for Black women to weigh more than women from other ethnic and racial groups carries across social class (Rand and Kuldau 1990; Williams 2002). While I do not believe that every overweight Black woman has an eating problem, I do maintain that "strong" Black women's tendencies to mask their emotions, frustrations, anger, and fears contribute to some of the weight they may carry through overeating, lack of regular exercise, or a general sense that focusing on their own needs is trivial or selfish. As a result, I wonder if strength were challenged both materially and ideologically whether African American women would still be among the most overweight, obese, and prone to debilitating and fatal weight-related diseases. When Black women feel empowered to enjoy their lives, to speak and be heard, and to choose their destinies, when they "learn *how* to put [their] needs first, [g]iving both Guilt and Struggle the finger" (Morgan 1999, 108), we may become compelled to adjust our expectations regarding weight and Black women.

4. Approximately 20–25% of American women will experience depression in their lives, and about 9% are depressed at any given time. Although 20% of depressed Americans receive treatment, as few as 7% of Black women do so (Mitchell and Herring 1998, 4). As I discuss in Chapter 4, most of the interviewees readily acknowledged that depression, both mild and clinical, was a reality among the Black women they knew. Their testimonies indicate that for reasons tied to the perception of depression as a white illness and incongruous with Black women's strength, there is much underreporting and little treatment of depression within this population. Such findings suggest the need to investigate depression as a gendered as well as racialized phenomenon.

5. As LaFrance (2007) points out, while the biomedical approach focused on neurotransmitters is most prominent in defining and treating depression in the United States, it is not the only explanatory or therapeutic model available. Like many feminist scholars attentive to women's lived experiences and the force of cultural discourses of femininity on women's psychological health, LaFrance (2007, 128) critiques the biomedical model, which "individualizes and depoliticizes distress, obscuring the 'depressing'

individual, social and political conditions of people's (and in particular women's) lives." Even when women—especially those who receive medical treatment—speak of biochemical sources to their distress, they largely discuss and place value on the psychosocial contexts that give rise to their feelings of being disconnected, frustrated, vulnerable, unwell, and in need of significant changes in their lives (LaFrance 2007; Schreiber and Hartrick 2002). Specifically, they identify imbalanced interpersonal relationships, overwhelming care demands, the structural powerlessness associated with poverty and immigration, sexual violence, and emotional abuse as each compromising their integrity (Cannon, Higginbotham, and Guy 1989; Schreiber 2001). However, because the integration of a fractured subjectivity is threatening to oppressive social orders, the pathologizing and medicalizing of depression are efforts of social control. While managing particular symptoms of depression, the quick adoption of a biomedical explanatory model greatly compromises women's ability to incorporate an understanding of the societal influences on their distress (Schreiber and Hartrick 2002, 100–101).

6. Throughout this book, I use the terms "depression," "depressive episodes," and "depressive experiences" interchangeably. I focus on Black women's subjective sense of periods in which they found themselves or other women unable to carry on with, and increasingly critical of, the demands of normative womanhood.

Chapter 3

1. A focus on strength raises questions about the frameworks through which racialized gender is promoted as a "tidy opposition" (Disch and Kane 1996, 290) in terms of Black and white womanhoods. While not the focus of this book, this problematic racialized dichotomy also renders the experiences of nonwhite and non-Black women theoretically invisible.

2. Black women often feel obliged to walk a fine line so that they are not characterized as either "too strong" or "weak." Both charges emerge from attempts to have them adhere to particular limits of racialized gender. "Too strong" is often a criticism leveled by men and women who subscribe to the notion that all women should be heterosexually coupled and sufficiently compliant in such relationships so as not to disparage the masculinity of men. "Weak" is generally an indictment of a Black woman who fails to demonstrate her distinctiveness from white womanhood, who suggests a frailty and a selfishness that stands in contrast to the perseverance and other-directedness of strength. What both terms reveal is the extreme power of external expectations on the goodness that Black women can claim.

3. The controlling image of the "angry Black woman" is a contemporary manifestation of Sapphire, "the archetypal nagging Black woman" (Mitchell

and Herring 1998, 56). Sapphire was a voiceful caricature whose complaints were typically dismissed as the ravings of a histrionic, inappropriate, and difficult woman. The "angry Black woman" or bitch is often a reference to behavior deemed "aggressive, loud, rude, and pushy" and uncomfortably non-middle-class (Hill Collins 2005, 123).

4. While Black women are often celebrated for having resilient women-centered relationships, few examples of such emerged in the data. Despite being in relationships with others (women kin and friends), the interviewees often felt that keeping up the appearance of being strong was essential to the workings of those bonds. As a result, they rarely sensed that they could reveal the doubts, fears, and resentments with which the performance of strength left them. In other words, such support did not allow them to take seriously and publicly discuss what they felt "deep down inside" or enable them to emerge beyond the social script of strength. I believe this seemingly aberrant finding is tied to a distinction that can be made between care and experiencing a kind of acknowledgment that allows one to reveal one's innermost thoughts without judgment. bell hooks (2000a) argues that within a national culture crafted out of patriarchal masculinity, consumption, and the denigration of people of color, we cannot but develop impoverished understandings of relatedness. Viewing love as a "verb" (4), she maintains that "affection is only one ingredient of love. To truly love we must learn to mix various ingredients—care, affection, recognition, respect, commitment, and trust, as well as honest and open communication" (5). The kinds of relationships to self and others that the women interviewed found sustaining, including Jennifer's sense of intrigue occasioned by the lesbian relationships she describes, were akin to hooks's definition of love. What this suggests is that if they were in loving relationships with others, the interviewees would have received not only material benefits and encouragement, but the support to question the received notions of male prerogative, black authenticity, and female self-sacrifice against which they privately railed.

Chapter 5

1. As investigated by The Harvard Project on Women's Psychology and the Development of Girls (Brown and Gilligan 1992; Gilligan [1982]1993; McLean Taylor, Gilligan, and Sullivan 1996), preadolescent girls demonstrate much awareness of the fraudulence of gender. In their own critiques of strength, hooks (1993), Scott (1991), and Wallace ([1978]1990) each appear to pinpoint a similar moment in girls' development when they see through this construction of racialized gender. This preadolescent critique is made most forcefully by Kesho Scott's daughters at the end of her 1991 book, *The Habit of Surviving*. Her eleven-year old, Jameka, centers on the dissemblance and

denial of vulnerability that characterize the strategy and expectation of strength. Of her mother and other strong Black women, Jameka writes, "I see a lot of black women covering something up. . . . I don't think it is good to cover up what's hurting you. . . . I want to be a black woman, but I don't want to end up like most of them—feeling responsible for everyone—and never being my own self and feeling like we always have to change something to make it better for our culture. It is too much pressure. I won't give in to it" (Scott 1991, 229, 231). The resistance of daughters to adopting their mothers' strength is a possibly rich focus for future research.

References

Alarcon, Norma. 1990. The theoretical subject(s) of this bridge called my back and Anglo-American feminism. In *Making face, making soul: Creative and critical perspectives by women of color*, ed. Gloria Anzaldua, 356–369. San Francisco: Aunt Lute Foundation.

Allan, Janet, Kelly Mayo, and Yvonne Michel. 1993. Body size values of white and Black women. *Research in Nursing and Health* 16:323–333.

Anderson, Kathryn and Dana Crowley Jack. 1991. Learning to listen: Interview techniques and analyses. In *Women's words: The feminist practice of oral history*, eds. Sherna Berger Gluck and Daphne Patai, 11–26. New York: Routledge.

Angelou, Maya. 2000. *Phenomenal woman*. New York: Random House.

Arnett Ferguson, Ann. 2001. *Bad boys: Public schools in the making of Black masculinity*. Ann Arbor: University of Michigan.

Bartky, Sandra Lee. 1990. *Femininity and domination: Studies in the phenomenology of oppression*. New York: Routledge.

Baturka, Natalie, Paige P. Hornsby, and John B. Schorling. 2000. Clinical implications of body image among rural African-American women. *Journal of General Internal Medicine* 15:235–241.

Beauboeuf-Lafontant, Tamara. 2003. Strong and large Black women? Exploring relationships between deviant womanhood and weight. *Gender & Society* 17:111–121.

————. 2005. Keeping up appearances, getting fed up: The embodiment of strength among African American women. *Meridians* 5:104–123.

————. 2007. "You have to show strength": An exploration of gender, race, and depression. *Gender & Society* 21:28–51.

————. 2008. Listening past the lies that make us sick: A voice-centered analysis of strength and depression in Black women. *Qualitative Sociology* 31:391–406.

Bell Kaplan, Elaine. 1997. *Not our kind of girl: Unraveling the myths of Black teenage motherhood.* Berkeley: University of California.

Bem, Sandra L. 1995. Working on gender as a gender-nonconformist. *Women & Therapy* 17:43–53.

Bordo, Susan. 1993. *Unbearable weight: Feminism, Western culture, and the body.* Berkeley: University of California.

Boyd, Julia A. 1998. *Can I get a witness? For sisters, when the blues is more than a song.* New York: Dutton.

Bray, Rosemary. 1992. Heavy burden. *Essence* 22 (January):52–54, 90–91.

Brown, Diane R. and Verna M. Keith. 2003. The epidemiology of mental disorders and mental health among African American women. In *In and out of our right minds: The mental health of African American women*, eds. Diane Brown and Verna Keith, 23–58. New York: Columbia University.

Brown, Lyn Mikel. 1998. *Raising their voices: The politics of girls' anger.* Cambridge, MA: Harvard University.

————. 2005. *Girlfighting: Betrayal and rejection among girls.* New York: New York University.

Brown, Lyn Mikel and Carol Gilligan. 1992. *Meeting at the crossroads: Women's psychology and girls' development.* New York: Ballantine.

Cannon, Lynn Weber, Elizabeth Higginbotham, and Rebecca F. Guy. 1989. *Depression among women: Exploring the effects of race, class, and gender.* Memphis, TN: Center for Research on Women, Memphis State University.

Carby, Hazel. 1987. *Reconstructing womanhood: The emergence of the Afro-American woman novelist.* New York: Oxford University.

Carlisle Duncan, Margaret and T. Tavita Robinson. 2004. Obesity and body ideals in the media: Health and fitness practices of young African-American women. *Quest* 56:77–104.

Chernin, Kim. [1982]1994. *The obsession: Reflections on the tyranny of slenderness.* New York: Harper Perennial.

Chu, Judy. 2005. Adolescent boys' friendship and peer group culture. *New Directions for Child and Adolescent Development* 107:7–22.

Clark Amankwaa, Linda. 2003a. Postpartum depression among African-American women. *Issues in Mental Health Nursing* 24:297–316.

———. 2003b. Postpartum depression, culture, and African-American women. *Journal of Cultural Diversity* 10:23–29.

———. 2005. Maternal postpartum role collapse as a theory of postpartum depression. *The Qualitative Report* 10:21–38.

Clark Hine, Darlene. 1989. Rape and the inner lives of Black women in the Middle West. *Signs* 14:912–920.

Cole, Elizabth R. and Safiya R. Omari. 2003. Race, class, and the dilemmas of upward mobility for African Americans. *Journal of Social Issues* 59:785–802.

Combahee River Collective. 1982. "A Black feminist statement." In *But some of us are brave*, eds. Gloria T. Hull, Patricia Bell Scott, and Barbara Smith, 13–22. Old Westbury, NY: Feminist Press.

Connell, Robert W. 1995. *Masculinities.* Berkeley: University of California.

Crenshaw, Kimberle. 1991. Mapping the margins: Intersectionality, identity politics, and violence against women of color. *Stanford Law Review* 43:1241–1299.

Crowley Jack, Dana. 1991. *Silencing the self: Women and depression.* Cambridge, MA: Harvard University.

———. 1999a. Silencing the self: Inner dialogues and outer realities. In *The interactional nature of depression*, eds. Thomas E. Joiner and James C. Coyne, 221–246. Washington, DC: American Psychological Association.

———. 1999b. *Behind the mask: Destruction and creativity in women's aggression.* Cambridge, MA: Harvard University.

———. 2003. The anger of hope and the anger of despair: How anger relates to women's depression. In *Situating sadness: Women and depression in social context*, eds. Janet Stoppard and Linda McMullen, 62–87. New York: New York University.

Danquah, Meri Nana-Ama. 1998. *Willow weep for me: An African American woman's journey through depression.* New York: One World.

Deutsch, Francine. 2007. Undoing gender. *Gender & Society* 21:106–127.

Disch, Lisa and Mary Jo Kane. 1996. When a looker is really a bitch: Lisa Olson, sport, and the heterosexual matrix. *Signs* 21:278–308.

Donovan, Roxanne and Michelle Williams. 2002. Living at the intersection: The effects of racism and sexism on Black rape survivors. *Women & Therapy* 25:95–105.

Dorsey, Allison. 2002. "White girls" and "Strong Black women": Reflections on a decade of teaching Black history at predominantly white institutions (PWIs). In *Twenty-first-century feminist classrooms: Pedagogies of identity and difference*, eds. Amie A. Macdonald and Susan Sanchez-Casal, 203–231. New York: Palgrave Macmillan.

DuBois, William E. Burghardt. 1903. *The souls of Black folk: Essays and sketches.* Chicago: A. C. McClurg.

DuCille, Ann. 2001. The colour of class: Classifying race in the popular imagination. *Social Identities* 7:409–419.

Duffy, Mignon. 2007. Doing the dirty work: Gender, race, and reproductive labor in historical perspective. *Gender & Society* 21:313–336.

Edge, Dawn and Anne Rogers. 2005. Dealing with it: Black Caribbean women's response to adversity and psychological distress associated with pregnancy, childbirth, and early motherhood. *Social Science and Medicine* 61:15–25.

Edmondson Bell, Ella J. and Stella M. Nkomo. 1998. Armoring: Learning to withstand racial oppression. *Journal of Comparative Family Studies* 29:285–295.

Foucault, Michel. 1977. *Discipline and punish: The birth of the prison*, trans. Alan Sheridan. New York: Vintage.

Friedan, Betty. [1963]1983. *The feminine mystique*. New York: Laurel.

Gillespie, Marcia Ann. [1978]1984. The myth of the strong Black woman. In *Feminist frameworks: Alternative theoretical accounts of the relations between women and men*, eds. Alison M. Jaggar and Paula S. Rothenberg, 32–35. New York: McGraw-Hill.

Gilligan, Carol. [1982]1993. *In a different voice: Psychological theory and women's development*. Cambridge, MA: Harvard University.

———. 1990. Prologue. In *Making connections: The relational worlds of adolescent girls at Emma Willard school*, eds. Carol Gilligan, Nona P. Lyons, and Trudy J. Hanmer, 1–5. Cambridge, MA: Harvard University.

———. 2003. *The birth of pleasure: A new map of love*. New York: Vintage.

———. 2006. When the mind leaves the body . . . and returns. *Deadalus* 135:55–66.

Gilligan, Carol, Renee Spencer, M. Katherine Weinberg, and Tatiana Bertsch. 2003. On the listening guide: A voice-centered, relational method. In *Qualitative research in psychology: Expanding perspectives methodology and design*, eds. Paul M. Camic, Jean E. Rhodes, and Lucy Yardley, 157–172. Washington, DC: American Psychological Association.

Grant, Linda. 1994. Helpers, enforcers, and go-betweens: Black females in elementary school classrooms. In *Women of color in U.S. society*, eds. Maxine Baca Zinn and Bonnie Thornton Dill, 43–63. Philadephia: Temple University.

Gray White, Deborah. [1985]1999. *Ar'n't I a woman? Female slaves in the plantation South*. New York: Norton.

———. 1999. *Too heavy a load: Black women in defense of themselves, 1894–1994*. New York: Norton.

Harris, Trudier. 1995. This disease called strength: Some observations on the compensating construction of Black female character. *Literature and Medicine* 14:109–206.

————. 2001. *Saints, sinners, saviors: Strong Black women in African American literature*. New York: Palgrave.

Harris-Lacewell, Melissa. 2001. No place to rest: African American political attitudes and the myth of black women's strength. *Women & Politics* 23:1–33.

Head, John. 2004. *Standing in the shadows: Understanding and overcoming depression in Black men*. New York: Broadway.

Hebl, Michelle and Todd Heatherton. 1997. The stigma of obesity in women: The difference is black and white. *Personality and Social Psychology Bulletin* 24:417–426.

Henson Scales, Meg. 2001. Tenderheaded, or rejecting the legacy of being able to take it. In *Tenderheaded: A comb-bending collection of hair stories*, eds. Juliette Harris and Pamela Johnson, 30–38. New York: Pocket Books.

Hesse-Biber, Sharlene. 1997. *Am I thin enough yet? The cult of thinness and the commercialization of identity*. New York: Oxford University.

Hill, Shirley A. 2005. *Black intimacies: A gender perspective on families and relationships*. Walnut Creek, CA: AltaMira Press.

Hill Collins, Patricia. 1998. *Fighting words: Black women and the search for justice*. Minneapolis: University of Minnesota.

————. 2000. *Black feminist thought: Knowledge, consciousness, and the politics of empowerment*. New York: Routledge.

————. 2005. *Black sexual politics: African Americans, gender, and the new racism*. New York: Routledge.

hooks, bell. 1981. *Ain't I a woman? Black women and feminism*. Boston: South End Press.

————. 1984. *Feminist theory: From margin to center*. Boston: South End Press.

————. 1989. *Talking back: Thinking feminist, thinking black*. Boston: South End Press.

————. 1991. Black women intellectuals. In *Breaking bread: Insurgent Black intellectual life*, eds. bell hooks and Cornel West, 147–164. Boston: South End Press.

————. 1993. *Sisters of the yam: Black women and self-recovery*. Boston: South End Press.

————. 2000a. *All about love: New visions*. New York: Harper Perennial.

————. 2000b. *Feminism is for everybody: Passionate politics*. Boston: South End Press.

————. 2001. *Salvation: Black people and love*. New York: Harper Perennial.

Hurtado, Aida. 1989. Relating to privilege: Seduction and rejection in the subordination of white women and women of color. *Signs* 14: 833–855.

Irvin Painter, Nell. 1996. *Sojourner Truth: A life, a symbol*. New York: Norton.

Johnson, Elon D. 2005. Miss Piggy gets depressed, too. In *Naked: Black women bare all about their skin, hair, lips, and other parts*, eds. Ayana Byrd and Akiba Solomon, 195–201. New York: Perigee.

Jones, Charisse and Kumea Shorter-Gooden. 2003. *Shifting: The double lives of Black women in America*. New York: Harper Collins.

Jordan, June. [1983]2000. Oughta be a woman. In *Home girls: A Black feminist anthology*, ed. Barbara Smith, xxix. New Brunswick, NJ: Rutgers University.

Joseph, Gloria I. 1981. Black mothers and daughters: Their roles and functions in American society. In *Common differences: Conflicts in Black and white feminist perspectives*, eds. Gloria I. Joseph and Jill Lewis, 75–126. Garden City, NY: Anchor.

King, Deborah K. 1988. Multiple jeopardy, multiple consciousness: The context of a Black feminist ideology. *Signs* 14:42–72.

LaFrance, Michelle. 2007. A bitter pill: A discursive analysis of women's medicalized accounts of depression. *Journal of Health Psychology* 12: 127–140.

LaFrance, Michelle and Janet Stoppard. 2006. Constructing a non-depressed self: Women's accounts of recovery from depression. *Feminism & Psychology* 16:307–325.

Leeds, Maxine. 1994. Young African-American women and the language of beauty. In *Ideals of feminine beauty: Philosophical, social, and cultural dimensions*, ed. Karen Gallagher, 147–159. Westport, CT: Greenwood.

Leigh, Wilhelmina A. and Daniele Huff. 2006. *Women of color health data book*. 3rd ed. Washington, DC: Office of Research on Women's Health, National Institutes of Health. http://orwh.od.nih.gov/pubs/Womenof Color2006.pdf (accessed April 7, 2008).

Litton Fox, Greer. 1977. "Nice girl": Social control of women through a value construct. *Signs* 2:805–817.

Lorde, Audre. 1984. Uses of the erotic: The erotic as power. In *Sister outsider: Essays and speeches by Audre Lorde*, 53–59. Berkeley, CA: Crossing Press.

Manring, Maurice M. 1998. *Slave in a box: The strange career of Aunt Jemima*. Charlottesville: University of Virginia.

Martin, Karin A. 2003. Giving birth like a girl. *Gender & Society* 17:54–72.

Martin, Marilyn. 2002. *Saving our last nerve: The African American woman's path to mental health*. Chicago: Hilton.

Marynick Palmer, Phyllis. 1983. White women/Black women: The dualism of female identity and experience in the United States. *Feminist Studies* 9:151–170.

Mauthner, Natasha. 2002. *The darkest days of my life: Stories of postpartum depression.* Cambridge, MA: Harvard University.

McLean Taylor, Jill, Carol Gilligan, and Amy M. Sullivan. 1996. *Between voice and silence: Women and girls, race and relationship.* Cambridge, MA: Harvard University.

Mitchell, Angela and Kennise Herring. 1998. *What the blues is all about: African American women overcoming stress and depression.* New York: Perigee.

Morgan, Joan. 1999. *When chickenheads come home to roost: My life as a hip-hop feminist.* New York: Simon & Schuster.

Morton, Patricia. 1991. *Disfigured images: The historical assault on Afro-American women.* Westport, CT: Praeger.

Moynihan, Daniel Patrick. 1965. *The Negro family: The case for national action.* Washington, DC: Office of Policy, Planning, and Research; United States Department of Labor.

Nakano Glenn, Evelyn. 1992. From servitude to service work: Historical continuities in the racial division of paid reproductive labor. *Signs* 1:1–43.

Neale Hurston, Zora. 1937. *Their eyes were watching God.* Greenwich, CT: Fawcett.

Okazawa-Rey, Margo, Tracy Robinson, and Janie Victoria Ward. 1987. Black women and the politics of skin color and hair. *Women & Therapy* 6:89–102.

Omolade, Barbara. 1994. *The rising song of African American women.* New York: Routledge.

Orbach, Susie. [1978]1988. *Fat is a feminist issue: The anti-diet guide to permanent weight loss.* New York: Berkeley Books.

Parker, Sheila, Mimi Nichter, Mark Nichter, Nancy Vuckovic, Colette Sims, and Cheryl Ritenbaugh. 1995. Body image and weight concerns among African American and white adolescent females: Differences that make a difference. *Human Organization* 54:103–114.

Perlick, Deborah and Brett Silverstein. 1994. Faces of female discontent: Depression, disordered eating, and changing gender roles. In *Feminist perspectives on eating disorders*, eds. Patricia Fallon, Melanie A. Katzman, and Susan C. Wooley, 77–93. New York: Guilford Press.

Phillips, Layli. 2006. Womanism: On its own. In *The womanist reader*, ed. Layli Phillips, xix–lv. New York: Routledge.

Powers, Retha. 1989. Fat is a black women's issue. *Essence* 20 (October):75, 78, 134, 136.

Pyke, Karen D. and Denise L. Johnson. 2003. Asian American women and racialized femininities: "Doing" gender across cultural worlds. *Gender & Society* 17:33–53.

Radford-Hill, Sheila. 2002. Keepin' it real: A generational commentary on Kimberly Springer's "third wave Black feminism." *Signs* 27:1083–1094.

Rand, Colleen S. W. and John M. Kuldau. 1990. The epidemiology of obesity and self-defined weight problem in the general population: Gender, race, age, and social class. *International Journal of Eating Disorders* 9:329–343.

Rich, Adrienne. 1980. Compulsory heterosexuality and lesbian existence. *Signs: Journal of Women in Culture and Society* 5:631–660.

Richardson, Mattie Udora. 2003. No more secrets, no more lies. *Signs* 15:63–76.

Richie, Beth. 1995. *Compelled to crime: The gender entrapment of battered, Black women*. New York: Routledge.

———. 2000. A Black feminist reflection on the antiviolence movement. *Signs* 25:1133–1137.

Ridgeway, Cecilia and Shelley Correll. 2004. Unpacking the gender system: A theoretical perspective on gender beliefs and social relations. *Gender & Society* 18:510–31.

Risman, Barbara J. 2004. Gender as a social structure: Theory wrestling with activism. *Gender & Society* 18:429–450.

Roberts, Dorothy. 1997. *Killing the Black body: Race, reproduction, and the meaning of liberty*. New York: Pantheon.

Rule Goldberger, Nancy. 1996. Cultural imperatives and diversity in ways of knowing. In *Knowledge, difference, and power: Essays inspired by Women's Ways of Knowing*, eds. Nancy Rule Goldberger, Jill Mattuck Tarule, Blythe McVicker Clinchy, and Mary Field Belenky, 335–371. New York: Basic Books.

Russell Hochschild, Arlie. 1979. Emotion work, feeling rules, and social structure. *The American Journal of Sociology* 85:551–575.

Schreiber, Rita. 1996. (Re)defining my self: Women's process of recovery from depression. *Qualitative Health Research* 6:469–491.

———. 1998. Clueing in: A guide to solving the puzzle of self for women recovering from depression. *Health Care for Women International* 19:269–288.

———. 2001. Wandering in the dark: Women's experiences with depression. *Health Care for Women International* 22:85–98.

Schreiber, Rita and Gwen Hartrick. 2002. Keeping it together: How women use the biomedical explanatory model to manage the stigma of depression. *Issues in Mental Health Nursing* 23:91–105.

Schreiber, Rita, Phyllis Noerager Stern, and Charmaine Wilson. 1998. The contexts for managing depression and its stigma among Black West Indian Canadian women. *Journal of Advanced Nursing* 27:510–517.

————. 2000. Being strong: How Black West-Indian Canadian women manage depression and its stigma. *Journal of Nursing Scholarship* 32:39–45.

Schrock, Douglas, Lori Reid, and Emily M. Boyd. 2005. Transsexuals' embodiment of womanhood. *Gender & Society* 19:317–335.

Scott, Kesho Yvonne. 1991. *The habit of surviving*. New York: Ballantine.

Shambley-Ebron, Donna Z. and Joyceen S. Boyle. 2006. In our grandmother's footsteps: Perceptions of being strong in African American women with HIV/AIDS. *Advances in Nursing Science* 29:195–206.

Shaw, Andrea. 2005. The other side of the looking glass: The marginalization of fatness and Blackness in the construction of gender identity. *Social Semiotics* 15:143–152.

Shorter-Gooden, Kumea and N. Chanell Washington. 1996. Young, Black, and female: The challenge of weaving an identity. *Journal of Adolescence* 19:465–475.

Siefert, Kristine, Phillip J. Bowman, Colleen M. Heflin, Sheldon Danziger, and David R. Williams. 2000. Social and environmental predictors of maternal depression in current and recent welfare recipients. *American Journal of Orthopsychiatry* 70:510–522.

Sizemore, Barbara A. 1973. Sexism and the Black male. *The Black Scholar* 4:2–11.

Smith, Barbara. 1998. *The truth that never hurts: Writings on race, gender, and freedom*. New Brunswick, NJ: Rutgers University.

Smith, Dorothy E. 1987. *The everyday world as problematic: A feminist sociology*. Boston: Northeastern University.

————. 1996. Telling the truth after postmodernism. *Symbolic Interaction* 19:171–202.

Stoppard, Janet. 2000. *Understanding depression: Feminist social constructionist approaches*. New York: Routledge.

Stoppard, Janet and Deanna Gammell. 2003. Depressed women's treatment experiences: Exploring themes of medicalization and empowerment. In *Situating sadness: Women and depression in social context*, eds. Janet Stoppard and Linda McMullen, 39–61. New York: New York University.

Taylor, Susan L. 1995. *Lessons in living*. New York: Anchor.

————. 1998. Taking back our power. *Essence* 29 (May):107

————. 2002a. God's perfect peace. *Essence* 33 (September):5.

————. 2002b. Passion for peace. *Essence* 33 (December):9.

Thompkins, Toby. 2004. *The real lives of strong Black women: Transcending myths, reclaiming joy*. Chicago: Agate.

Thompson, Becky. 1994. *A hunger so wide and so deep: American women speak out on eating problems*. Minneapolis: University of Minnesota.

————. 1996. "A way outa no way": Eating problems among African American, Latina, and white women. In *Race, class, and gender: Common bonds, different voices*, eds. Esther Ngan-Ling Chow, Doris Wilkinson, and Maxine Baca Zinn, 52–69. Thousand Oaks, CA: Sage.

Tolman, Deborah. 1994. Doing desire: Adolescent girls' struggles for/with sexuality. *Gender & Society* 8:324–342.

————. 2002. *Dilemmas of desire: Teenage girls talk about sexuality.* Cambridge, MA: Harvard University.

Townsend Gilkes, Cheryl. 2001. *"If it wasn't for the women . . .": Black women's experience and womanist culture in church and community.* Maryknoll, NY: Orbis.

Ussher, Jane. 2004. Premenstrual syndrome and self-policing: Ruptures in self-silencing leading to increased self-surveillance and blaming of the body. *Social Theory and Health* 2:254–272.

Vera, Hernan, Joe R. Feagin, and Andrew Gordon. 1995. Superior intellect? Sincere fictions of the white self. *Journal of Negro Education* 64:295–306.

Walcott-McQuigg, Jacqueline A., Judith Sullivan, Alice Dan, and Barbara Logan. 1995. Psychosocial factors influencing weight control behavior of African American women. *Western Journal of Nursing Research* 17:502–520.

Wallace, Michele. [1978]1990. *Black macho and the myth of the superwoman.* New York: Verso.

————. 1990. *Invisibility blues: From pop to theory.* New York: Verso.

Ward, Janie Victoria. 1996. Raising resisters: The role of truth telling in the psychological development of African American girls. In *Urban girls: Resisting stereotypes, creating identities*, eds. Bonnie Ross Leadbeater and Niobe Way, 85–116. New York: New York University Press.

————. 2000. *The skin we're in: Teaching our children to be emotionally strong, socially smart, spiritually connected.* New York: Fireside.

Weedon, Chris. [1987]1997. *Feminist practice and poststructuralist theory.* 2nd ed. Malden, MA: Blackwell.

Weems, Renita. 2004. Sanctified and suffering. *Essence* 35 (December):160–162, 164.

Welsh, Kariamu. 1979. I'm not that strong. *Essence* 9 (February):39.

West, Candace and Don H. Zimmerman. 1987. Doing gender. *Gender & Society* 1:125–151.

Williams, David R. 2002. Racial/ethnic variations in women's health: The social embeddedness of health. *American Journal of Public Health* 92:588–597.

Williamson, Lisa. 1998. Eating disorders and the cultural forces behind the drive for thinness: Are African American women really protected? *Social Work in Health Care* 28:61–73.

Wolf, Naomi. 1991. *The beauty myth: How images of beauty are used against women*. New York: William Morrow.

Wu, Frank. 2003. *Yellow: Race in America beyond Black and white*. New York: Basic Books.

Index

Angry Black woman, 91–92, 166–167n3. *See also* Controlling images

Bordo, Susan, 48
Breakdowns, 67; as Black women's term for depression, 45, 65, 125–127, 143. *See also* Depression
Brown, Lyn Mikel, 9–10

Chernin, Kim, 47, 152
Clark Hine, Darlene, 39–40
Compulsive overeating, 49, 51–57, 68, 109–119, 140, 165n3; gender ambivalence and, 48, 52; as muted protest, 132; sexual abuse and, 119–121. *See also* Eating problems; Internalization
Compulsory heterosexuality, 84
Controlling images: definition of, 22; "good" womanhood and, 46; matrix of domination and, 21–22; racialized gender and, 24, 152; strength as, 18, 25–35, 105. *See also*

Angry Black woman; Hegemonic femininity; Jezebel; Mammy; Strength; Strong Black woman
Crowley Jack, Dana, 57–60, 162n5, 164n1

Depression: anger and, 164n1; biomedical approach to, 165–166n5; denial of among Black women, 64–66, 128–131; divided consciousness and, 59–60, 131–132; gender ambivalence and, 46–48; healing from, 60; as muted protest, 132; prevalence of, 62, 165n4; as racialized and gendered phenomenon, 61–66; self-silencing and, 19; strength discourse and, 38, 61–66, 68, 121–131. *See also* Breakdowns; Silencing paradigm of women's depression
Discourse: definition of, 7; subjectivity and, 7–11. *See also* Strength
Dissemblance, 39–42, 56, 95–104, 126, 167–168n1; depression and, 62, 126;

Tamara Beauboeuf-Lafontant is Associate Professor of Sociology and Education Studies at DePauw University. She is co-editor of *Facing Racism in Education,* 2nd edition.